5th Workshop on Speech and Language Processing for Assistive Technologies

(SLPAT 2014)

Held at ACL 2014

Baltimore, Maryland, USA
26 June 2014

ISBN: 978-1-63439-199-3

Printed from e-media with permission by:

Curran Associates, Inc.
57 Morehouse Lane
Red Hook, NY 12571

Some format issues inherent in the e-media version may also appear in this print version.

Printed by Curran Associates, Inc. (2014)

For permission requests, please contact the Association for Computational Linguistics
at the address below.

Association for Computational Linguistics
209 N. Eighth Street
Stroudsburg, Pennsylvania 18360

Phone: 1-570-476-8006
Fax: 1-570-476-0860

acl@aclweb.org

Additional copies of this publication are available from:

Curran Associates, Inc.
57 Morehouse Lane
Red Hook, NY 12571 USA
Phone: 845-758-0400
Fax: 845-758-2634
Email: curran@proceedings.com
Web: www.proceedings.com

Introduction

We are pleased to bring you the Proceedings of the Fifth Workshop on Speech and Language Processing for Assistive Technologies (SLPAT), held in Baltimore, US on 26 June 2014. We received 9 paper submissions, of which 7 were chosen for oral presentation. In addition, we have also accepted special talks *Technology Tools for Students With Autism: Innovations That Enhance Independence and Learning* by K.I. Boser, M. Goodwin, and S.C. Wayland, and *Dysarthria as a noisy channel in speech production* by Frank Rudzicz.

This workshop is intended for researchers from all areas of speech and language technology with a common interest in making everyday life more accessible for people with physical, cognitive, sensory, emotional, or developmental disabilities. This workshop builds on four previous such workshops (co-located with NAACL HLT 2010, EMNLP in 2011, NAACL HLT 2012, and Interspeech 2013), as well as the previously held SMIAE workshop (co-located with ACL 2012). The workshop provides an opportunity for individuals from research communities, and the individuals with whom they are working, to share research findings, and to discuss present and future challenges and the potential for collaboration and progress.

While augmentative and alternative communication (AAC) is a particularly apt application area for speech and natural language processing (NLP) technologies, we purposefully made the scope of the workshop broad enough to include assistive technologies (AT) as a whole, even those falling outside of AAC. While we encouraged work that validates methods with human experimental trials, we also accepted work on basic-level innovations and philosophy, inspired by AT/AAC related problems. Thus we have aimed at broad inclusivity, which is also manifest in the diversity of our Program Committee.

We would like to thank all the people and institutions who contributed to the success of the SLPAT 2014 workshop. Finally, we would like to thank the Association for Computational Linguistics (ACL) for support in preparing and run the workshop.

Jan Alexandersson, Dimitra Anastasiou, Cui Jian, Ani Nenkova, Rupal Patel, Frank Rudzicz, Annalu Waller, Desislava Zhekova

Co-organizers of SLPAT 2014

Organizing committee:

Jan Alexandersson, DFKI, Germany
Dimitra Anastasiou, University of Bremen, Gernany
Cui Jian, SFB/TR 8 Spatial Cognition, University of Bremen, Germany
Ani Nenkova, University of Pennsylvania, USA
Rupal Patel, Northeastern University, USA
Frank Rudzicz, Toronto Rehabilitation Institute and University of Toronto, Canada
Annalu Waller, University of Dundee, Scotland
Desislava Zhekova, University of Munich, Germany

Program committee:

Cecilia Ovesdotter Alm, Rochester Institute of Technology, USA
Jean-Yves Antoine, Université François-Rabelais, France
John Arnott, University of Dundee, UK
Véronique Aubergé, CNRS/Laboratoire d'Informatique de Grenoble, France
Melanie Baljko, York University, Canada
Janice Bedrosian, Western Michigan University, USA
Stefan Bott, Universitat Pompeu Fabra, Spain
Annelies Braffort, CNRS/LIMSI, France
Torbjørg Breivik, Language Council of Norway
Francesco Buccafurri, University of Reggio Calabria, Italy
Tim Bunnell, Speech Research Lab, duPont Hospital for Children, USA
Corneliu Burileanu, University Politehnica of Bucharest, Romania
Heidi Christensen, University of Sheffield, UK
Heriberto Cuayahuitl, Heriot-Watt University, UK
Stuart Cunningham, University of Sheffield, UK
Nina Dethlefs, Heriot-Watt University, UK
Rickard Domeij, Swedish Language Council, Sweden
Eleni Efthimiou, Institute for Language and Speech Processing (ILSP) / R.C. "Athena", Greece
Michael Elhadad, Ben-Gurion University, Israel
Alain Franco, Nice University Hospital, France
Evita Fotinea, Institute for Language and Speech Processing (ILSP) / R.C. "Athena", Greece
Thomas Francois, University of Louvain, Belgium
Corinne Fredouille, Université d'Avignon/LIA, France
Kathleen Fraser, University of Toronto, Canada
Corinne Fredouille, Université d'Avignon et des Pays du Vaucluse, France
Jort Gemmeke, KU Leuven, Belgium
Kallirroi Georgila, University of Southern California, USA
Stefan Götze, Fraunhofer Institute for Digital Media Technology, Germany
Björn Granström, Royal Institute of Technology, Sweden
Phil Green, University of Sheffield, UK

Charlie Greenbacker, University of Delaware, USA
Mark Hasegawa-Johnson, University of Illinois, USA
Per-Olof Hedvall, Lund University, Sweden
Rubén San Segundo Hernández Technical University of Madrid, Spain
Jeff Higginbotham, University at Buffalo, USA
Graeme Hirst, University of Toronto, Canada
Linda Hoag, Kansas State University, USA
Matt Huenerfauth, CUNY, New York, USA
Sofie Johansson Kokkinakis, University of Gothenburg, Sweden
Simon Judge, Barnsley NHS & Sheffield University, UK
Per Ola Kristensson, University of St. Andrews, UK
Sandra Kübler, Indiana University, USA
Benjamin Lecouteux, Université Pierre Mendés-France/LIG, France
Greg Lesher, Dynavox Technologies Inc., USA
William Li, MIT, USA
Peter Ljunglöf, University of Gothenburg and Chalmers University of Technology, Sweden
Eduardo Lleida, University of Zaragoza, Spain
Ilias Maglogiannis, University of Central Greece, Greece
Diana McCarthy, University of Cambridge, UK
Kathleen McCoy, University of Delaware, USA
Ornella Mich, Fondazione Bruno Kessler, Italy
Yael Netzer, Ben-Gurion University, Israel
Alan Newell, Dundee University, UK
Torbjørn Nordgård, Lingit A/S, Norway
Rupal Patel, Northeastern University, USA
Francois Portet, Laboratoire d'informatique de Grenoble, France
Joseph Reddington, University of London, UK
Luz Rello, Universitat Pompeu Fabra, Spain
Brian Roark, Google, USA
Niels Schütte, Dublin Institute of Technology, Ireland
Richard Sproat, Google, USA
Kristina Striegnitz, Union College, USA
Kumiko Tanaka-Ishii, Kyushu University, Japan
Thora Tenbrink, Bangor University, UK
Nava Tintarev, University of Aberdeen, UK
Keith Vertanen, Montana Tech of The University of Montana, USA
Nadine Vigouroux, Université Paul Sabatier/IRIT, France
Tonio Wandmacher, SYSTRAN, Paris, France
Karl Wiegand, Northeastern University, USA
Sandra Williams, The Open University, UK
Maria Wolters, University of Edinburgh, UK

Table of Contents

Conference Program

Thursday, June 26, 2014

9:00–9:15	Welcome & Opening Remarks
	Session 1
09:14–09:45	*Standing on the shoulders of giants: attacking the meta-problems of technical AAC research* Joseph Reddington
09:45–10:15	*Graphical Modification of Text. An Approach To Dyslexic Users.* Tereza Pařilová
10:15–10:30	Break
	Session 2
10:30–11:00	Special Talk by K.I. Boser, M. Goodwin, and S.C. Wayland: *Technology Tools For Students With Autism: Innovations That Enhance Independence and Learning*
11:00–11:30	*Dialogue Strategy Learning in Healthcare: A Systematic Approach for Learning Dialogue Models from Data* Hamidreza Chinaei and Brahim Chaib-draa
11:30–12:00	*Speech recognition in Alzheimer's disease with personal assistive robots* Frank Rudzicz, Rosalie Wang, Momotaz Begum and Alex Mihailidis
12:00–14:00	Lunch

Thursday, June 26, 2014 (continued)

Standing on the shoulders of giants: attacking the meta-problems of technical AAC research

Joseph Reddington
joe@joereddington.com

Abstract

Augmentative Alternative Communication (AAC) policy suffers from a lack of large scale quantitative evidence on the demographics of users and diversity of devices.

The 2013 Domesday Dataset was created to aid formation of AAC policy at the national level. The dataset records purchases of AAC technology by the UK's National Health Service between 2006 and 2012; giving information for each item on: make, model, price, year of purchase, and geographic area of purchase. The dataset was designed to help answer open questions about the provision of AAC services in the UK; and the level of detail of the dataset is such that it can be used at the research level to provide context for researchers and to help validate (or not) assumptions about everyday AAC use.

This paper examine three different ways of using the Domesday Dataset to provide verified evidence to support, or refute, assumptions, uncover important research problems, and to properly map the technological distinctiveness of a user community.

1 Introduction

Technical researchers in the AAC community are required to make certain assumptions about the state of the community when choosing research projects that are calculated to make the most effective use of research resources for the greatest possible benefit.

A particular issue is estimating how easily technical research can achieve wide scale adoption or commercial impact. For example, (Szekely et al., 2012) uses a webcam and facial analysis to allow a user to control expressive features of their synthetic speech by means of facial expressions. Such work is clearly useful, but it is difficult to assess its potential commercial impact without also knowing what proportion of currently available AAC devices include webcams and how that proportion is changing over time. Similarly, corpus based approaches such as (Mitchell and Sproat, 2012) could potentially be brought to market very quickly, but that potential can only be assessed if we also have some awareness of the range and popularity of AAC devices that either have space for such a corpus or the internet capability to access one. Unfortunately, even though there are a range of AAC focused meta-studies in the literature (see, for example, (Pennington et al., 2003; Pennington et al., 2004; Hanson et al., 2004; Alwell and Cobb, 2009)) they give little information on the technical landscape of AAC.

This paper examines three issues of interest to technical researchers in AAC, each from a different stage in the research lifecycle. It then shows how the Domesday Dataset (Reddington, 2013) can provide evidence to support, or refute, assumptions, uncover important research problems, and map the technological distinctiveness of a user community.

This paper is structured as follows, Section 2 introduces the Domesday Dataset and discusses the context it is used in in this work. Section 3 examines the issue that little is known about the prevalence of equipment within the AAC user community, and because of this lack of information it is difficult to establish baselines, or contexts. We

Proceedings of the 5th Workshop on Speech and Language Processing for Assistive Technologies (SLPAT), pages 1–8,
Baltimore, Maryland USA, August 26 2014.

show how the Domesday Dataset can allow researchers to ground their assumptions in empirical data.

Section 4 examines a cultural shift in AAC technology. The arrival of the iPad and other tablets in the field has caused a great deal of change and it is unclear what the long term implications will be. We believe it is important to provide hard data on the direct economic changes that have occurred in the marketplace. The Domesday Dataset allows us to examine the number of physical devices purchased before and after the tablet explosion.

Section 5 examines the issue of transferability. It is assumed by many AAC professionals that the ability for AAC users to transfer page sets between different devices is a significant issue for AAC users. This section first shows how we can derive some context information from the Domesday Dataset and goes on to discuss the sociotechnical context of the problem space.

2 The Domesday Dataset

In 2013 the Domesday Dataset was created to aid formation of AAC policy at the national level. The dataset records purchases of AAC technology by the UK's National Health Service between 2006 and 2012; giving information on make, model, price, year of purchase, and geographic area of purchase for each item. It was formed by submitting freedom of information requests to every NHS (National Health Service) trust asking for details of all AAC devices provided since 2006. The requests required the year of purchase, make, and manufacture of each device. The full details of the construction are reported in (Reddington, 2013).

At the time of writing, the Domesday Dataset contained details of 9,157 purchases from NHS Trusts. (Reddington, 2013) estimates that the trusts that have responded cover approximately 90% of the UK population. All versions of the dataset are held online and licensed under an Open Data Commons Attribution License. The dataset meets the requirements for three star linked open data according to (Berners-Lee, 2010). A sample of information appearing in the Domesday Dataset is given in Table 1. The dataset was not only intended to shape UK policy and research, but also as a snapshot for international researchers: allowing comparison of manufacturers, types of aids, budgets, and prevalence within a tight geographical domain.

There are, of course, caveats to consider before using the Domesday Dataset. Firstly, for privacy reasons, it is presented with no connection to any other element of AAC provision: it is impossible to match equipment with a particular user.

Secondly, the NHS does not have the complete information: information from AAC manufacturers shows that only 44% of sales and 38% of the spend were by the NHS. Even with complete data from the public bodies, researchers would be forced to extrapolate the information, perhaps confirming the trends by means of another research methodology. This work makes the assumption that the relative frequency of AAC purchases and trends in the UK are reflected in the dataset. We are careful not to over-analyse this information, but we do note that having a complete list of NHS purchases, even if they only cover 44% of a county's purchases, is vastly more detailed than any previous record of AAC provision. Potential problems with the dataset underrepresenting tablet sales are discussed in Section 4.

3 Research Granularity

Little is known about the prevalence of equipment within the AAC user community, and because of this lack of information it is difficult to establish baselines, or contexts. Perhaps worse, when researchers propose solutions, they must also make a range of assumptions about the applicability of their work to the wider AAC audience. We can, for example, imagine an innovative new model for AAC not being successful because it requires a consistent internet connection from the device, which perhaps only 5% of users have. The majority of AAC research is devoted to building up a library of case studies to show the benefits of AAC for user groups. This focus on social issues in AAC research is laudable, and vital for the overall area; however, researchers working in the assistive technology field would be more effective if they could answer direct questions about need, capability and technology. For example, a researcher who must choose between supporting a project that reduces errors in word-prediction using eye-gaze by 20%, or a project that makes Step-By-Step devices more responsive and intuitive to use for children, faces a difficult choice without evidence. If the researcher could check that in a particular geographic area there were 45 eye-gaze systems and nearly 600 Step-by-Steps, then that

Purchase year	Manufacturer	Model	Num.	Unit Price	Total Price
2006	Liberator	E-Tran Frame	1	£120.00	£120.00
2006	Servox	Digital Electronic Larynx	2	£520.00	£1,040.00
2006	Ablenet	Armstrong Mount	1	£190.00	£190.00
2006	Ablenet	Big Mack	6	£84.00	£504.00
2007	Inclusive	Switchit "Bob the Builder"	1	£49.00	£49.00
2007	Cricksoft	Crick USB Switch Box	2	£99.00	£198.00
2007	Sensory Software	Joycable2	1	£49.00	£49.00
2007	Dynavox	Boardmaker	1	£209.00	£209.00
2007	ELO	LCD Touch Monitor	1	£419.00	£419.00
2008	Ablenet	iTalk2 Communication Aid	2	£95.00	£190.00
2008	Attainment Company Inc	Go Talk(unknown type)	4	£130.00	£520.00
2008	Aug. Communication Inc.	Talking Photo Album	2	£18.91	£37.82

Table 1: Extract from the Domesday Dataset, taken from (Reddington, 2013) (Geograpic information held seperately)

might influence the decision[1] (at a higher level this is, of course, the calculation that one expects funding bodies to make when awarding the grants that allow projects to even begin). Having quantitative manufacturing data also supports much more general estimations of research impact, as well as helping research groups evaluate possible commercial partners.

Even within the United States, which is the major market for manufacturers, and the most active area for AAC research, the complexities of its healthcare system, differing state legislation, and disability culture make estimation difficult. Even the strong efforts that have been made (Matas et al., 1985; Bloomberg and Johnson, 1990; Binger and Light, 2006; Huer, 1991) give estimations of need and use, but none that can be expected to give the granularity that technologists need for their investigation, or even to frame research questions.

3.1 What Domesday tells us

To illustrate the use of the Domesday Dataset for technical researchers, we give some simple results regarding the popularity of various types of AAC device. Table 2 shows the list of most common 'high tech' AAC purchases by the NHS in Scotland, ordered by the number of units purchased between 2006 and 2012. Table 3 gives the same table for purchases in England. Both tables are based on a relatively open definition of 'high tech' AAC: these lists include only devices that can produce a range of different utterances, and allow those utterances to be selected by icon, or keyboard. As a result they do not include such devices as, for example: Big Macks; Digital Electronic Larynxs; Jelly Bean Twists; Step–by-Steps; MegaBees and many others, which are included in the Domesday Dataset. As discussed in Section 2 we do not advise the direct quoting of these figures without first being familiar with the caveats discussed in (Reddington, 2013). The figures should be considered comparative only.

Rank	Model	Units
1	Lightwriter (SL35/SL40)	37
2	GoTalk (all types)	34
3	iPads and iPods	15
4	Springboard Lite	12
5	Vantage Lite	6
6	SuperTalker	6
7	Dynamo	6
8	V Max	5
9	Tech/Speak 32 x 6	4
10	Liberator 14	4
11	C12 + CEYE	4

Table 2: The 11 most common 'high tech' speech aids purchased by the NHS in Scotland 2005-2011

Some of the more counter-intuitive results from Tables 2 and 3 include the general absence (with the notable exception of the iPad/iPod) of touch screen devices. Indeed, both the Lightwriter and the GoTalk range comfortably sell more than twice as many units as their nearest touchscreen rival.

A more sobering result to consider for researchers in technical AAC is the popularity of

[1] In either direction of course, depending on the weighting given to a variety of other factors.

Rank	Model	Units
1	Lightwriter (SL35/SL40)	77
2	GoTalk (all types)	74
3	iPad/iPod/iPhone	29
4	Springboard Lite	27
5	V Max	11
6	Dynamo	10
7	SuperTalker	7
8	Vantage Lite	6
9	Tech/Speak 32 x 6	6
10	Chatbox	5
11	C12 + CEYE	4

Table 3: The 11 most common 'high tech' speech aids purchased by the NHS in England 2005-2011

devices that are less obvious targets for customisation and improvement. The GoTalk and Tech/Speak ranges are solid favourites for a particular section of the market and part of their appeal is that they are relatively 'non-technical'[2] and are much easier for users and staff to get to grips with: this appeal is somewhat in tension with advanced features like automatic generation of content and voice banking. It is entirely possible that technical research would have more impact if it focuses on making high-capability devices more acceptable to existing users rather than increasing the already impressive capability of existing devices.

Another aspect of interest is the speed at which the AAC market changes with respect to the existing landscape. The Dynavox Dynamo, for example, is a popular device in both tables, but it has been discontinued for some time. Section 5 explores some of the issues that this situation can raise. Finally we consider that there are some systems that we would have expected to appear in these lists that are absent: for example, Dynavox's Xpress and Maestro or Tobii's MyTobii, and Liberator's Nova. Speculating on why some products become more popular is beyond the scope of this work; however, we do consider it an area for future interest.

This section has shown that examining the Domesday Dataset at even the most basic level identifies a range of factors that can help contextualise the technical landscape for researchers in AAC. To return to the examples given in the introduction, we can see how it would be simple for (Szekely et al., 2012) to use the iPod and iPad's position in the marketplace as evidence for the potential of their work and we can see how corpus based approaches such as (Mitchell and Sproat, 2012) can use the range of AAC devices with internet connections to inform the design process. We note that as the data covers a five year period it is possible to examine 'fashions' as purchases rise and fall and even map the gradual spread geographically.

4 Tablets and other animals

This section examines the extent to which the introduction of tablet-based AAC has altered the user community at the technical level and discusses how this data can be used by technical researchers.

Since 2010, when Apple released the iPad, there have been major upheavals in the AAC market, caused by the explosion in tablet computing. From an engineering perspective, the iPad only suffers in comparison to existing devices in terms of ruggedness; however, at potentially one quarter the price[3], it is comparatively replaceable. From a software perspective the iPad gives many 'cottage industry' developers for AAC a low cost way to enter the market. Such developers already include Alexicom, TapToTalk, AssistiveWare, and over 100 others. Such developers are well placed to take advantage of the platform's underlying hardware.

Apples's position as a top-tier technology giant, along with the iPad's position as the dominant tablet platform can be seen as a serious change to the AAC industry as a whole. However, for many working within the AAC community, it is unclear what the long term implications will be. Apple represents the most successful of a large group of companies such as Samsung, HP, and (via the Android operating system, and the purchase of Motorola) Google (Weber, 2011) that have invested heavily in tablet technology. It is conceivable that one or more manufacturers will develop a 'ruggedised' tablet for military or medical use. Such a tablet, particularly if using the Android operating system, which has a large group of dedicated AAC developers (Higginbotham and Jacobs, 2011), would open a 'second front' from the point of view of the existing manufacturers, as it would

[2]For example, neither device has a LCD screen, instead they have buttons with printed icons

[3]Based on estimates from (Reddington, 2013)

remove many of the perceived weaknesses of the iPad (fragility, waterproofing, volume).

The picture is muddied greatly because neither the major AAC manufacturers nor Apple release reliable sales figures. This results in the uncomfortable situation for users, professionals, and researchers alike, that we are simultaneously being told that "The iPad is simply the flavour of the month at the moment and it is just the effect of hype" and "The major manufacturers simply can't compete at any level other than eye-gaze".

Of course, the issue of the overall effectiveness of tablet-based AAC must be paramount for the general AAC community, and there is a large amount of research resources investigating this. This paper simply attempts to provide some hard data on the technical changes that have occurred in the marketplace since 2010.

4.1 Domesday on tablet AAC

If we assume an average lifespan of four years per device, then Table 2 and Table 3 can be considered to give a reasonable approximation of the relative popularity of AAC devices currently active in the UK AAC community. As discussed in Section 3, touchscreen and other high-capability devices are not dominating the market, but we can deduce that Apple devices have a strong market share compared to devices with similar capabilities. In Table 2 and Table 3 iPads and other Apple devices are shown to be approximately even in terms of units shipped with established touchscreen systems such as the Springboard Lite. It would be difficult to argue that Apple devices were not a major part of the AAC landscape.

A factor in these estimations must be the relatively recent explosion in table computing. If we limit our data to only purchases since 2010 (as shown in Table 4), we see that Apple devices dominate the sector and we would expect that when the Domesday Dataset is extended in 2014, we shall see that Apple devices have achieved the position of market leader in terms of AAC devices in use.

4.1.1 Other tablets

We note that, other than some appearances of the FuturePad Windows system (running Grid 2 software and predating the tablet explosion), there are no tablet purchases in the dataset that are not an Apple device. This is a somewhat unexpected find: the Android app store shows hundreds of thousands of downloads (worldwide) for AAC applications for the Android platform. Some potential explanations for this tension are discussed in the following section, but we consider this an area for future research.

4.1.2 Potential understatement of tablet sales

Section 2 discussed some caveats about information in the Domesday Dataset, in particular that it only examines purchases in the medical sector and is understood to cover less than half of the AAC market. We note here that these caveats may disproportionately affect tablet computing purchases. For example, the relatively low cost of tablet devices means that there is a growing possibility that the paradigms used by service providers are no longer fit for purpose. Whereas previous paradigms may have involved users waiting two years for a £7000 communication aid, with £3000 worth of support and training, the same users may now, out of desperation, opt to pay out of their own pocket for a £700 tablet with 'app'. In terms of the goals of this paper, such situations artificially depress the recorded purchases of tablet devices, and in terms of the goals of the AAC community, the choice of a 'better device later or cheaper device now' may not be to the long term benefit of users, or society.

Moreover, we can also imagine situations where tablet devices are already present in an AAC user's life before they become used as a dedicated device. In the same way that family members often 'hand down' older phones to parents or children when they upgrade, we have anecdotal evidence of situations were "Chris can try an app on Steve's old iPad while he is at university and then we'll buy Steve a new one if that works". Such practices would again artificially depress the number of purchases recorded.

In this work we concentrate on only the reports of purchase of physical tablets. Although the Domesday Dataset does contain app purchases where they have been recorded by the NHS, the wide range of AAC applications, both free and paid for, and their transferability between devices mean that only the most vague of comparisons could be made.

Even without these caveats, it is clear from examination of the Domesday Dataset that, in the UK at least, Apple devices like the iPad have become a large part of the technical AAC landscape and we note that their level of hardware and strong developer communities make them attractive tar-

Rank	Model	Units
1	iPad/iPod/iPhone	25
2	GoTalk (all types)	10
3	Lightwriter (SL35/SL40)	10
4	Springboard Lite	6
5	EC02	6
6	C12 + CEYE	3
7	SuperTalker	2
8	Dynavox Maestro	2
9	Powerbox 7	2
10	S5	2
11	Dynavox (type unknown)	2

Table 4: The 11 most common 'high tech' speech aids purchased by the NHS in England 2010-2011

gets for researchers building prototype AAC devices.

5 Transferability of data

It is assumed by many AAC professionals that *transferability*, the ability for AAC users to transfer page sets between different devices, is a significant issue for AAC users. Unfortunately there is no previous academic research to support this in general or estimate the size of the problem space. This section first shows how we can derive some contextual information from the Domesday Dataset and goes on to discuss the sociotechnical context of the problem space.

We can examine the set of devices purchased in the years 2006-2012 and check to see if they were still available to purchase in 2012. From this we can estimate the lifespan of each device to extract the set of devices that are 'irreplaceable' in the sense that the same model cannot be purchased in cases of loss.

A large proportion of the devices listed in the Domesday Dataset are no longer available to buy[4]; however, they are still in service and, in some cases, still in manufacturer's warranty. The resulting set of irreplaceable devices is large and this information supports a need for more research.

These irreplaceable devices contextualise a space in which a range of sociotechnical issues at the social and economic level have special resonance with the AAC user community (for work examining the reliability of AAC devices and their likely length of time before needing repairs please see, for example, (Shepherd et al., 2009; Ball et al., 2007)).

As discussed in (Reddington and Coles-Kemp, 2011; Coles-Kemp et al., 2011), the custom utterances and user history on a device form not only a large part of the user's way of interacting with the world, but often, their memories and sense of self.

It is recognised by manufacturers that this data is precious and many manufacturers of electronic AAC systems offer the functionality to back up the devices to external storage. However, in the event of irrecoverable hardware failure, such backups are only generally useful if the user's replacement device is of the same model as the existing device (in some cases, manufacturers can transfer backups between different models of the same manufacturer). If it is the case that an AAC device's functional lifespan is longer than the device sales lifespan, then it is also the case that massive information loss must occur when a range's devices reach the end of their lifespan and users are shifted onto other devices.

Moreover, because AAC device backups are not held in a common format, it is difficult for AAC users to transfer sets of pages between devices at all. If a user wishes to switch from, say Proloque2go to Dynavox, then the only way to transfer potentially key parts of their identity and memory between the devices is for the user, or care staff, to laboriously recreate systems by hand. This results in users having difficulties 'trying out' new systems, and the occasional sight of a user with two AAC devices: one that is failing but has the full range of utterances, and a more modern device that may be clearer and more effective, but which does not yet have all the necessary utterances. Finally, the lack of a common format stands as a barrier to the deployment of a truly 'open source' page and symbol set that could be used across formats and developed independently of hardware manufactures.

It is the author's position that this shows a clear and present need for not only a standardised format for transferring sets of pages between devices but also that this standardised format be open and accessible to researchers. We consider these to be a counterpart of the work in (Deruyter et al., 2007); however, where (Deruyter et al., 2007) focused on increased interoperability between AAC and mainstream technologies, we argue in favour

[4]The Domesday Dataset has examples from major manufactures that include the DV4, the Dynamo, the Vanguard, the Springboard, and many others.

of increased interoperability between the devices themselves. The work is perhaps philosophically closer to the work of (Lesher et al., 2000b; Lesher et al., 2000a), which seeks to produce universal standards of logging of AAC utterances for research purposes. We argue that a standardised format would also allow technical researchers to develop their prototypes to interface directly with a user's existing systems. This would produce a much more seamless way of testing innovations, without the need to introduce users to dedicated equipment or a specialised app for testing a particular innovation in AAC technology.

6 Discussion

Research in AAC policy and technology suffers greatly from a lack of large scale quantitative evidence on the prevalence of devices, and the demographics of users. This work has shown that the Domesday Dataset can be used at the research level to provide context for researchers and to help validate (or not) assumptions about everyday AAC use. This work examined three different issues of interest to technical researchers in AAC, each from a different stage in the research lifecycle. It provided a case study in using the dataset to gain an understanding of the level of technology currently deployed in the UK AAC community, and exposed a number of open research questions.

This work also gave an analysis of the impact of the explosion in tablet computing on the AAC technological landscape. We provided evidence that Apple devices are already a significant part of the AAC community and that we expect their presence to grow as older devices phase out of the market.

Finally we considered how the Domesday Dataset suggests that product function lifespan may be longer than the product sales lifespan in AAC technology and discussed the consequences of this from a sociotechnological perspective. This work has pushed the AAC research agenda in a direction more attractive to larger studies, commercial manufactures, and quantitative research to support the traditionally qualitatively focused field. The range of possibilities for AAC research includes: more accurate estimates of populations of AAC users, and levels of AAC use; the ability to evaluate the potential impact of research prototypes and methodologies; and the ability to examine those sectors of the AAC industry that have been most successful at delivering improved functionality to users.

6.1 Future research agenda

At the more fundamental level we hope that this work encourages public debate about where the trade-offs lie in terms of targeting technical research in both AAC and the wider intellectual disability field. It is the author's position that stakeholders at all levels in AAC should be involved in debate on the areas of focus for research resources.

Moreover, we believe that an open format for transferring sets of pages between devices is needed, and that such a format will improve both user experience, commercial competition, and research effectiveness. We would welcome further work.

Acknowledgments

This research was made possible by the large range of contributors to the construction of the Domesday Dataset, including staff at Toby Churchill and Liberator Ltd. We also thank, Pam Enderby, Alex John, Sarah Creer, and the team at Sheffield University, along with Tom Bamber at Loughborough University, and Selina Sutton at Newcastle University.

References

Morgen Alwell and Brian Cobb. 2009. Social and communicative interventions and transition outcomes for youth with disabilities a systematic review. *Career Development for Exceptional Individuals*, 32(2):94–107.

Laura J Ball, David R Beukelman, Elizabeth Anderson, Denise V Bilyeu, Julie Robertson, and Gary L Pattee. 2007. Duration of aac technology use by persons with als. *Journal of Medical Speech Language Pathology*, 15(4):371.

Tim Berners-Lee. 2010. Linked data. Personal website ('http://www.w3.org/DesignIssues/LinkedData.html'), Jun.

Cathy Binger and Janice Light. 2006. Demographics of preschoolers who require aac. *Language, Speech, and Hearing Services in Schools*, 37(3):200.

Karen Bloomberg and Hilary Johnson. 1990. A statewide demographic survey of people with severe communication impairments. *Augmentative and Alternative Communication*, 6(1):50–60.

L. Coles-Kemp, J. Reddington, and P.A.H. Williams. 2011. Looking at clouds from both sides: The advantages and disadvantages of placing personal narratives in the cloud. *Information Security Technical Report*, 16(3):115–122.

Frank Deruyter, David McNaughton, Kevin Caves, Diane Nelson Bryen, and Michael B Williams. 2007. Enhancing aac connections with the world. *Augmentative and Alternative Communication*, 23(3):258–270.

EK Hanson, KM Yorkston, and DR Beukelman. 2004. Speech supplementation techniques for dysarthria: a systematic review. *Journal of Medical Speech Language Pathology*, 12.

Jeff Higginbotham and Steve Jacobs. 2011. The future of the android operating system for augmentative and alternative communication. *Perspectives on Augmentative and Alternative Communication*, 20(2):52–56.

Mary Blake Huer. 1991. University students using augmentative and alternative communication in the usa: A demographic study. *Augmentative and Alternative Communication*, 7(4):231–239.

Gregory W Lesher, Bryan J Moulton, Gerard Rinkus, and D Jeffery Higginbotham. 2000a. *A universal logging format for augmentative communication*. Citeseer.

Gregory W Lesher, Gerard J Rinkus, Bryan J Moulton, and D Jeffery Higginbotham. 2000b. Logging and analysis of augmentative communication. In *Proceedings of the RESNA Annual Conference*.

Judy Matas, Pamela Mathy-Laikko, David Beukelman, and Kelly Legresley. 1985. Identifying the nonspeaking population: A demographic study. *Augmentative and Alternative Communication*, 1(1):17–31.

Margaret Mitchell and Richard Sproat. 2012. Discourse-based modeling for aac. In *Proceedings of the Third Workshop on Speech and Language Processing for Assistive Technologies*, pages 9–18, Montréal, Canada, June. Association for Computational Linguistics.

Lindsay Pennington, Juliet Goldbart, and Julie Marshall. 2003. Speech and language therapy to improve the communication skills of children with cerebral palsy. *Cochrane Database of Systematic Reviews*, 3.

Lindsay Pennington, Juliet Goldbart, and Julie Marshall. 2004. Interaction training for conversational partners of children with cerebral palsy: a systematic review. *International Journal of Language & Communication Disorders*, 39(2):151–170.

J. Reddington and L. Coles-Kemp. 2011. Trap hunting: Finding personal data management issues in next generation aac devices. *Proceedings of the second workshop on speech and language processing for assistive technologies*, pages 32–42.

Joseph Reddington. 2013. The Domesday dataset: linked and open data in disability studies. *Journal of Intellectual Disabilities*, 17(2):107–121.

Tracy A Shepherd, Kent A Campbell, Anne Marie Renzoni, and Nahum Sloan. 2009. Reliability of speech generating devices: A 5-year review. *Augmentative and Alternative Communication*, 25(3):145–153.

Eva Szekely, Zeeshan Ahmed, Joao P. Cabral, and Julie Carson-Berndsen. 2012. Winktalk: a demonstration of a multimodal speech synthesis platform linking facial expressions to expressive synthetic voices. In *Proceedings of the Third Workshop on Speech and Language Processing for Assistive Technologies*, pages 5–8, Montréal, Canada, June. Association for Computational Linguistics.

Tim Weber. 2011. BBC News - Google to buy Motorola Mobility, last retrieved September 2011.

Graphical Modification of Text. An Approach To Dyslexic Users.

Tereza Pařilová
Faculty of Informatics
Masaryk University
Botanická 68a, Brno 602 00, Czech Republic
parilova@mail.muni.cz

Abstract

The requirements of user interface for dyslexics have not been yet properly explored. Accessibility to any kind of information or just to entertainment web pages is a key factor to equality of rights, moreover it breaks down social barriers. Considering that study materials are nowadays very much accessible through internet, by accommodating web content to anyhow disabled users must be seen as natural thing. Dyslexia is considered as an cognitive impairment arising from visual similarity of letters, therefore we focus on Czech language which uses special characters. The aim of our research is to introduce an application that allows dyslexics to decode text easier and understand it properly.

1 Introduction

Unlike for blind or deaf people, it is quite difficult to identify requirements for users with dyslexia, as they are very individual. The dyslexics' inability to decode information is socially restrictive as much as the inability of visually impaired to read the information (Deibel, 2006). For more, missing one sense is balanced by higher sensitivity of other senses. But dyslexics do not miss a sense.

According to psycho-linguistic studies (Marshall and Newcombe, 1973; Friedman et al., 2012), the words in text should not contain more letters (or letters close to each other) that are visually similar. It counts letters like *b, p, d, o, q* etc. Also, dyslexics find very hard encoding words that are too long for them. Such a word should be broken up by linguistic or visual syllable, depending on the order of problematic symbols. In Czech language it might be: *nej-roz-ší-ře-něj-ší* instead of nejrozšířenější ("the most widely used", by linguistic syllable, too long word), *kap-oun* instead of *ka-poun* etc. ("fish", visually). The finding, reported in Proceedings of the National Academy of Sciences (Siok et al., 2008) surprisingly shows that there is significant difference in ability to decode words in different languages.

2 Related Work

The main elements causing reading inability dwells in visual attention deficit and letter concentration, both based in neural cognition. Research that was done with eye tracker shows that at least one third of probands have difficulties with catching text with eyes (Bellocchi et al., 2013). The same results are indicated in independent study of Laboratory for visual Learning at the Smithsonian Astrophysical Observatory (Schneps et al., 2013).

For instance mobile application American Wordspeller & Phonetic Dictionary helps users to check their writing and converts phonetic spelling into the proper one. Other software that use text to speech conversion, so that users do not have to deal with visual matter, are Web Reader and CapturaTalk. In past year, IDEAL, the e-book reader was introduced by Rello (2012). Anyway, this application is not a solution for modifying too long words or words with a combination of wrong letters. Moreover, Czech language is too complicated to get by with IDEAL application.

Most of the applications use text to speech conversion approach for its usefulness and simplicity. However, reading should not be avoided by dyslexics. The research study

Proceedings of the 5th Workshop on Speech and Language Processing for Assistive Technologies (SLPAT), pages 9–12,
Baltimore, Maryland USA, August 26 2014.

conducted by experts from the Institute of Education, University of London shows that reading strenghts attention, brain cognition and information processing over time (Battye and Rainsberry, 2013). Therefore, an application based on text modification is very much needed.

3 The Complexity of the Czech Language

Czech language belongs to West Slavic language class. It is inflected language, characterized by a complicated system of declension and conjugation. According to the complexity and a huge vocabulary, the use of applications for instance offering synonyms seems not usable. The declension and conjugation that affects nouns and verbs are grammatical tasks that makes the language and assistive applications most complicated.

3.1 Declension

Czech speakers typically refer to the noun cases by number and learn them by means of the question and answer (Šaur, 2004). These numbers do not necessarily correspond to numbered cases in other languages. Nouns, adjectives, pronouns and numbers are declined, there are seven cases over a number of declension models (Tab. 1).

3.2 Conjugation

Conjugation applies to verbs. It is a system of grammatically-determined modifications. There are several types of conjugation with more or less complicated rules. A brief overview is in Tab. 2.

Table 1. Declension of Czech nouns.

case	question	title
1	who/what?	nominative
2	without whom/what?	genitive
3	to whom/what?	dative
4	We see whom/what?	accusative
5	We address/call	vocative
6	about whom/what?	locative
7	with whom/what?	instrumental

Table 2. Conjugation of Czech verbs.

Affection	Types/Classes
Infinitive	
Participles	Past/Passive
Transgressive	
Aspect	Perfect/Imperfect
Tense	Present/Past/Future
Imperative	Singular/Plural
Conditionals	Present/Past
Passive voice	
Reflexive verbs	
Negation	
Verb Classes	1 – 5
Irregular Verbs	

3.3 Phonetical and Grammatical Syllables

Czech language, as it was stated, is a quit hard language with many words that follow declension and conjugation. It is still under linguistic concern how to divide syllables in Czech words. There are rules that often do not follow natural feelings of those speaking Czech, respectively those whose Czech is a mother language (Moravec-Robur, 1939). Automatic syllabication is therefore still not flawless and there may be accidental errors that would make dyslexics even more confused. Moreover, phonological syllable does not omit proximity of problematic letters that are hardly decodable.

4 Methodology

4.1 Experimental Approach

We introduce an application that modifies text according to needs of Czech language environment.

Because the complexity of words depends on individual language, we have to find out the pattern that makes the Czech words hard to decode. We prepare sets of text, one that is original and contains general, non-scientific words, one that divides the letters according to linguistic syllables and the last one that divides the letters in words according to visual syllables.

Original text:
Pomněnky nekvetou na podzim, ale kvetou pouze z jara.

Phonetic (grammatical) syllables:
Po-mněn-ky nekvetou na pod-zim, ale kvetou pou-ze z jara.

Visual syllables:
Pom-něnky nekvetou na p-o-dzim, ale kvetou p-ouze z jara.

Figure 1. The three texts read by dyslexics.

Each set has 3 texts which are similar in length. To avoid subjectivity, the proband cannot be tested with same text but we need the texts to be similar as much as possible (Fig. 1). The dyslexics read the three texts, not told what the aim of the experiment is. We measure how fast the dyslexic read each text while the text is read loudly to avoid distorting elements like skipping letters, returning etc. The text with phonological (grammatical) syllables divides the letters only in words they appear in. For exact measurement we use a system reacting on sound so while the dyslexic start reading, the tool starts measuring and stops when the last letter is read.

4.2 Technical Approach

Among observation, we need a tool that will detect long words and visually similar letters in the words (according to above mentioned pattern). For modifying the text we use syntactic analyzer that looks for symbols given in a rule that was set according to general text reading problems. For instance, a diagram using cyclical algorithm defines the way to detect such words/letters (Fig. 2). The tool will be built up using state machine.

To the system in Figure 2, if NIS is for example ≥ 2, the word is possibly hard to decode and has to be broken up into syllables or visually not similar groups of letters. For instance a word "podobná" has more than 2 problematic letters close to each other (there are 5 problematic letters together – p+o+d+o+b) so the letters in the word should be broken up at least after two of such letters (po-do-bná), better after each of the letter (p-o-d-o-bná), depending on preset rule for each language. The same way we detect number of letters contained in a single word.

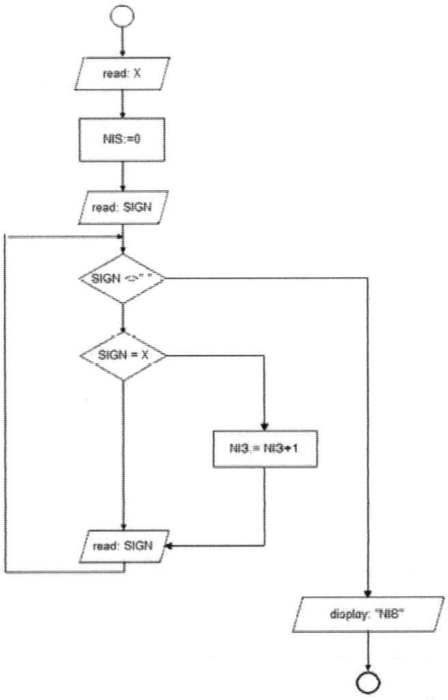

Figure 2. Cyclical algorithm for detecting problematic words.

The only need is to determine what letters, respectively what pair or triplet of letters are problematic for exact language. Once the observation is done, the application we design can be used for any language.

5 Scientific and Practical Impact

Based on previous work that was done in area of dyslexic users, within psychological, linguistic and technical studies, we strongly believe that our solution fits best to dyslexics who are very individual users to work with. There are no standards, like WCAG 2.0 for general accessibility that would make web designers and ICT developers to follow such needs. First, they would have to care about accommodating these needs in every single webpage, ebook, ICT tool. It seems impossible, too hard and time consuming. Second, designers and developers have almost none of experience with dyslexic users and self-experience is more than needed when building an assistive technology tool.

We believe that our research, proving explicit problems that dyslexics deal with, will move the research in assistive technologies far more ahead. Existing applications are helpful but do not fulfill the needs as much as they could. We add value to actual applications and make the gap between society and people with special needs smaller.

6 Conclusion

The outcome of the application is necessary to confront with a sufficient group of dyslexics. It is generally stated that up to one twentieth of population suffers from learning and concentration disabilities, although only some of them are diagnosed (Rello et al., 2013). It would be unethical to stop having interests in problematic with dyslexia.

Our future work will be directed the way of developing proposed tool, to make it usable in e-books, study materials, and within daily routine needs.

References

Claire Battye and Meghan Rainsberry, 2013. *Reading for pleasure puts children ahead in the classroom, study finds.* Institute of Education, University of London.

Guarang Kanvind, Luz Rello and Ricardo Baeza-Yatez, 2012. *IDEAL: a Dyslexic-Friendly eBook Reader.* Proceedings of the 14th international ACM SIGACCESS conference on Computers and accessibility. ACM, New York, NY, USA, 205-206.

John C. Marshall and Freda Newcombe, 1973. *Patterns of paralexia: A psycholinguistic approach.* Journal of Psycholinguistic Research. Kluwer Academic Publishers-Plenum Publishers, 2(3):175-199.

Katherine Deibel, 2006. *Understanding and supporting the use of accommodating technologies by adult learners with reading disabilities.* Accessibility and Computing, ACM SIGACCESS, 86: 32-35.

Luz Rello, Ricardo Baeza-Yates, Stefan Bott and Horacio Saggion, 2013. *Simplify or help?: text simplification strategies for people with dyslexia.* Proceedings of the 10th International Cross-Disciplinary Conference on Web Accessibility , ACM New York, NY, (15).

Mattheew H. Schneps, Jenny M. Thomson, Chen Chen, Gerhard Sonnert and Marc Pomplun, 2013. *E-Readers Are More Effective than Paper for Some with Dyslexia.* PLoS ONE 8(9):e75634

Naama Friedmann, Michal Biran and Aviah Gvion, 2012. *Patterns of visual dyslexia.* Journal of Neuropsychology, 6(1):1–30.

Stefon Bellocchi, Mathilde Muneaux, Mireille Bastien-Toniazzo and Sébastien Ducrot, 2013. *I can read it in your eyes: What eye movements tell us about visuo-attentional processes in developmental dyslexia.* Research in Developmental Disabilities, 34(1):452-460.

Vladimír Šaur, 2004. *Rules of Czech spelling grammar with interpretation.* Otto Publishing, Prague.

Wai T. Siok, Zhendong Niu, Zhen Jin, Charles A. Perfetti and Li H. Tan. 2008. A structural–functional basis for dyslexia in the cortex of Chinese readers. Massachusetts Institute of Technology, Cambridge, MA, USA, 105(14):5561–5566.

Dialogue Strategy Learning in Healthcare: A Systematic Approach for Learning Dialogue Models from Data

Hamid R. Chinaei
Hamidreza.Chinaei.1@ulaval.ca

Brahim Chaib-draa
Brahim.Chaib-Draa@ift.ulaval.ca

Abstract

We aim to build dialogue agents that optimize the dialogue strategy, specifically through learning the dialogue model components from dialogue data. In this paper, we describe our current research on automatically learning dialogue strategies in the healthcare domain. We go through our systematic approach of learning dialogue model components from data, specifically user intents and the user model, as well as the agent reward function. We demonstrate our experiments on healthcare data from which we learned the dialogue model components. We conclude by describing our current research for automatically learning dialogue features that can be used in representing dialogue states and learning the reward function.

1 Introduction

Cognitive assistive technologies provide support systems for the elderly, possibly with cognitive or physical disabilities, for instance people with dementia (such as Alzheimer's disease) (Boger et al., 2005; Pineau et al., 2011; Rudzicz et al., 2012). Such support systems can significantly reduce the costs of performing several tasks, currently done by family members or employed caregivers. In this context, (Rudzicz et al., 2012) are working on a computerized caregiver that assist individuals with Alzheimer's disease (AD) to complete daily tasks (e.g., preparing meals) using verbal communication. Thus, an important component of such technologies is the dialogue agent.

Table 1 (left) shows sample dialogues collected by SmartWheeler, an intelligent wheelchair for persons with disabilities (Pineau et al., 2011). In particular, SmartWheeler aims to minimize the physical and cognitive load required in steering it. SmartWheeler is equipped with a dialogue agent, thus the users can give their commands through the spoken language besides a joystick.

The first line denoted by u_1 shows the true user utterance, which is the one that has been extracted manually from user audio recordings. The following line denoted by $\tilde{u}_1$ is the recognized user utterances by automatic speech recognition (ASR). Finally, the line denoted by a_1 shows the performed action in response to the ASR output at the time of collecting the dialogues. First, the users may say a command in different ways. For instance for turning right, the user may say *turn right a little please*, *turn right*, *right a little*, or *right*.

Furthermore, challenges can occur when ASR output is imperfect. That is, for each dialogue utterance recognized by ASR, the dialogue agent must estimate the human user intent and then to perform the best action that satisfies the user intent. The recognized utterance by ASR is not reliable for decision making. For instance, the first utterance, u_1: "turn right a little", shows the true user utterance. The ASR output for this utterance is, $\tilde{u}_1$: [10 writer little]. As such, the action performed by SmartWheeler at this dialogue turn is, the general query action u_1: PLEASE REPEAT YOUR COMMAND.

We are working on automatically learning the dialogue strategy by learning the dialogue model components such as user intents, dialogue features, and the agent's reward function from data. Our data includes dialogues between human users and expert agents (such as caregivers).

2 Theoretical approach

Sequential Decision Making: Figure 1 shows the cycle of interaction between an agent (such as a dialogue agent or a caregiver) and its environment (such as a human user). The agent performs an action and receives an observation in return. The observation can be used by the agent, for in-

Proceedings of the 5th Workshop on Speech and Language Processing for Assistive Technologies (SLPAT), pages 13–19,
Baltimore, Maryland USA, August 26 2014.

u_1 :	turn right	u_1 :	turn right
$\tilde{u}_1$:	[turn right]	$\tilde{u}_1$:	[turn right]
a_1 :	TURN RIGHT	s_1 :	*turn-right-little, 60%*
u_2 :	turn right a little	u_2 :	turn right a little
$\tilde{u}_2$:	**[10 writer little]**	$\tilde{u}_2$:	**[10 writer little]**
a_2 :	**PLEASE REPEAT YOUR COMMAND**	s_2 :	***turn-right-little, 90%***
u_3 :	turn right a little	u_3 :	turn right a little
$\tilde{u}_3$:	[turn right to lead a]	$\tilde{u}_3$:	[turn right to lead a]
a_3 :	TURN RIGHT A LITTLE	s_3 :	*turn-right-little, 90%*
u_4 :	stop	u_4 :	stop
$\tilde{u}_4$:	[stop]	$\tilde{u}_4$:	[stop]
a_4 :	STOP	s_4 :	*stop, 90%*

Table 1: Left: A sample from the SmartWheeler dialogues (Pineau et al., 2011). Right: results of learning human user intents from patients' noisy dialogues.

stance to update its state and reward. The reward works as reinforcement from the environment that shows how well the agent performed. In sequential decision making, the agent is required to make decision for sequence of states rather than making a one-shot decision. Then, the sequential decision making is performed with the objective of maximizing the long term rewards. The sequence of actions is called a strategy, and the major question in sequential decision making is how to find a near optimal strategy.

Reinforcement learning (RL): RL in (partially observable) Markov decision processes, so called the (PO)MDPs, is a learning approach in sequential decision making. In particular, (PO)MDPs have been successfully applied in dialogue agents (Roy et al., 2000; Zhang et al., 2001; Williams, 2006; Thomson and Young, 2010; Gašić, 2011). The (PO)MDP framework is a formal framework to represent uncertainty explicitly while supporting automated strategy solving. Specifically, it is an optimization framework that supports automated strategy solving by maximizing a "reward function".

3 Objective

SDS (Spoken dialogue system) researchers have addressed several practical challenges of applying (PO)MDPs to SDS (Williams, 2006; Paek and Pieraccini, 2008). Specifically, estimating the user model and the reward function is a significant challenge since these model components have a direct impact on the optimized dialogue strategy. Furthermore, the reward function is perhaps the most hand-crafted aspect of the optimization frameworks such as (PO)MDPs (Paek and Pieraccini, 2008). Using *inverse reinforcement learning* (IRL) techniques, a reward function can be determined from expert actions (such as caregiver actions) (Ng and Russell, 2000). Fortunately, learning the reward function using IRL methods have already been proposed for the general (PO)MDP framework (Ng and Russell, 2000; Kim et al., 2011), paving the way for investigating its use for dialogue (PO)MDPs. In this context, the IRL algorithms require dialogue features (for instance ASR recognitions with their confidence scores) for representing the reward function. Extracting relevant dialogue features is important since the dialogue features and their representation highly affect the learned reward function and finally the optimized strategy.

Thus, our goals include building (PO)MDP-based dialogue technologies that optimizes the dialogue strategy through learning user intents and the user model, and reward function from dialogue data, as follows:

1. Learning user intents and the user model from collected dialogues, i.e., ASR recognitions, or directly from acoustic data.
2. Learning the reward function.
   (a) Learning useful dialogue features.
   (b) Representing features in IRL for learning the reward function.

Recall Figure 1 that shows the cycle of interaction between an agent (such as a dialogue agent or a caregiver) and its environment (such as a human user). In this figure, circles represent the learned models. The model denoted by (PO)MDP includes the (PO)MDP model components, without

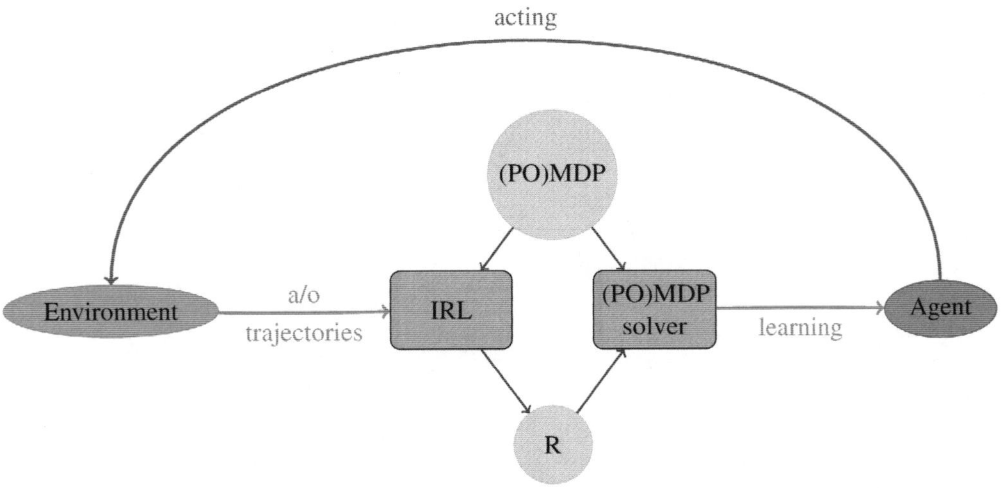

Figure 1: The cycle of acting/learning between the agent and environment. The circles represent the models. The model denoted by (PO)MDP includes the (PO)MDP model components, without a reward function, learned from step 1 in the objective section. The learned (PO)MDP model together with expert action/observation trajectories are used in IRL to learn the reward function denoted by R, in step 2 in the objective section. The learned (PO)MDP and reward function are used in the (PO)MDP solver to learn/update the strategy.

a reward function, which have been learned from step 1 above. The learned (PO)MDP together with action/observation trajectories are used in IRL to learn the reward function, denoted by R. Then, the learned (PO)MDP and the reward function are used in a (PO)MDP solver to learn/update the optimal strategy.

4 SmartWheeler data

The SmartWheeler project aims to build an intelligent wheelchair for persons with disabilities (Pineau et al., 2011). In particular, SmartWheeler aims to minimize the physical and cognitive load required in steering it. This project has been initiated in 2006, and a first prototype, shown in Figure 2, was built in-house at McGill's Center for Intelligent Machines.

We used the dialogues collected by SmartWheeler to develop dialogue (PO)MDPs, learned primarily from data. The data includes eight dialogues with healthy users and nine dialogues with target users of SmartWheeler (Pineau et al., 2011). The dialogues with target users, who are the elderly, are somehow more noisy than the ones with healthy users. More specifically, the average word error rate (WER) equals 13.9% for the healthy user dialogues and 18.5% for the target user dialogues. In order to perform our experiments on a larger amount of data, we used all the healthy and target user dialogues. In total, there are 2853 user utterances and 422 distinct words in the SmartWheeler dialogues.

Figure 2: The SmartWheeler robot platform (Pineau et al., 2011).

5 Learning user intents from data

We learned the (PO)MDP states by learning the user intents occurred in the dialogue set using a topic modeling approach, i.e., Hidden Topic

Markov Model (HTMM) (Gruber et al., 2007). HTMM is a variation of Latent Dirichlet Allocation (LDA) which learns topics from text based on co-occurrence of words and using Dirichlet distribution for generating the topics of text documents (Blei et al., 2003). HTMM adds Markovian assumption to the LDA model in order to exploit the Markovian property between sentences in the documents. Thus, HTMM can be seen both as a variation of Hidden Markov Model (HMM) and a variation of LDA.

Our experimental results showed that HTMM learns proper user intents that can be used as dialogue states, and is able to exploit the Markovian property between dialogue utterances, adequately. The learned states, using our proposed methods, from SmartWheeler data are as follows: s_1 : *move-forward-little*, s_2 : *move-backward-little*, s_3 : *turn-right-little*, s_4 : *turn-left-little*, s_5 : *follow-left-wall*, s_6 : *follow-right-wall*, s_7 : *turn-degree-right*, s_8 : *go-door*, s_9 : *set-speed*, s_{10} : *follow-person*, s_{11} : *stop*. Table 3 shows the learned user intents, five of them, with their top-four words, i.e., the intent *keywords*.

Table 1 (right) shows results of HTMM application on SmartWheeler for the example shown in Table 1 (left). For instance, the second utterance shows that the user actually uttered *turn right a little*, but it is recognized as *10 writer little* by ASR. The most probable intent returned by HTMM for this utterance is s_3 *: turn-right-little* with 90% probability. This is because HTMM considers Markovian property for deriving intents. As a result, in the second turn it estimates correctly the true user intent based on the user intent in the first turn.

The list of all SmartWheeler actions are shown in Table 2. Each action is the right action of one state (the user intent for a specific command). So, ideally, there should be 24 states for SmartWheeler dialogues (There are 24 actions other than the general query action: REPEAT). However, we only learned 11 of the states, mainly because of the number of dialogues. That is, not all of the states appeared in the data frequently enough. There are also states that do not appear in dialogues at all.

a_1	DRIVE FORWARD A LITTLE
a_2	DRIVE BACKWARD A LITTLE
a_3	TURN RIGHT A LITTLE
a_4	TURN LEFT A LITTLE
a_5	FOLLOW THE LEFT WALL
a_6	FOLLOW THE RIGHT WALL
a_7	TURN RIGHT DEGREE
a_8	GO THROUGH THE DOOR
a_9	SET SPEED TO MEDIUM
a_{10}	FOLLOW THE WALL
a_{11}	STOP
a_{12}	TURN LEFT
a_{13}	DRIVE FORWARD
a_{14}	APPROACH THE DOOR
a_{15}	DRIVE BACKWARD
a_{16}	SET SPEED TO SLOW
a_{17}	MOVE ON SLOPE
a_{18}	TURN AROUND
a_{19}	PARK TO THE RIGHT
a_{20}	TURN RIGHT
a_{21}	DRIVE FORWARD METER
a_{22}	PARK TO THE LEFT
a_{23}	TURN LEFT DEGREE
a_{24}	PLEASE REPEAT YOUR COMMAND

Table 2: The list of the possible actions, performed by SmartWheeler.

6 Learning reward functions from data

In this section, we experiment our implementation of the trajectory-based MDP-IRL algorithm proposed by (Ng and Russell, 2000). The IRL experiments are designed to verify if the introduced IRL methods are able to learn a reward function for the expert strategy, where the expert strategy is represented as a (PO)MDP strategy. That is, the expert strategy is the strategy that the underlying (PO)MDP framework optimizes. The MDP expert strategy for each of the (PO)MDP state is represented in Table 4. This strategy suggests performing the right action of each state.

6.1 MDP-IRL learned rewards

We applied the MDP-IRL algorithm on SmartWheeler dialogue MDP described above using the introduced keyword features in Table 5. The algorithm was able to learn a reward function in which the strategy equals the expert strategy for all states, (the expert strategy shown in Table 4). Table 6 shows the learned reward function. Note that, for instance for state s_3: *turn-right-little*, the reward of performing both actions a_3: TURN RIGHT A LITTLE and a_4: FOLLOW THE RIGHT WALL is close to 1. Nevertheless, the optimized strategy for this reward function suggest the correct action, i.e., TURN RIGHT A LITTLE for this state (*turn-right-little*).

intent 1		*intent 2*		*intent 3*		*intent 4*		...		*intent 11*	
forward	18.0%	**backward**	38.0%	**right**	20.9%	**left**	18.9%			**stop**	94.2%
move	16.1%	drive	33.3%	turn	17.1%	turn	17.1%			stopp	02.2%
little	11.4%	little	10.9%	little	13.1%	little	13.8%			scott	00.7%
drive	08.1%	top	01.7%	bit	07.4%	right	09.0%	...	...	but	00.2%
...	...	...	...	...	...	...	...			...	...

Table 3: The learned user intents from the SmartWheeler dialogues and their top words. Each percentage shows the probability of each word given the intent.

state	state description	expert action	expert action description
s_1	*move-forward-little*	a_1	DRIVE FORWARD A LITTLE
s_2	*move-backward-little*	a_2	DRIVE BACKWARD A LITTLE
s_3	*turn-right-little*	a_3	TURN RIGHT A LITTLE
s_4	*turn-left-little*	a_4	TURN LEFT A LITTLE
s_5	*follow-left-wall*	a_5	FOLLOW THE LEFT WALL
s_6	*follow-right-wall*	a_6	FOLLOW THE RIGHT WALL
s_7	*turn-degree-right*	a_7	TURN RIGHT DEGREES
s_8	*go-door*	a_8	GO THROUGH THE DOOR
s_9	*set-speed*	a_9	SET SPEED TO MEDIUM
s_{10}	*follow-wall*	a_{10}	FOLLOW THE WALL
s_{11}	*stop*	a_{11}	STOP

Table 4: The learned strategy using the learned dialogue MDP from SmartWheeler dialogues.

	forward	backward	**right**	**left**	turn	go	for	top	stop
s_1	1	0	0	0	0	0	0	0	0
s_2	0	1	0	0	0	0	0	0	0
s_3	0	0	**1**	0	0	0	0	0	0
s_4	0	0	0	**1**	0	0	0	0	0
s_5	0	0	0	**1**	0	0	0	0	0
s_6	0	0	**1**	0	0	0	0	0	0
s_7	0	0	0	0	1	0	0	0	0
s_8	0	0	0	0	0	1	0	0	0
s_9	0	0	0	0	0	0	1	0	0
s_{10}	0	0	0	0	0	0	0	1	0
s_{11}	0	0	0	0	0	0	0	0	1

Table 5: Keyword features for the SmartWheeler dialogues.

	a_1	a_2	a_3	a_4	a_5	a_6	a_7	a_8	a_9	a_{10}	a_{11}	a_{12}	...	REPEAT
s_1	1.0	0	0	0	0	0	0	0	0	0	0	0	...	0
s_2	0	1.0	0	0	0	0	0	0	0	0	0	0	...	0
s_3	0	0	**1.0**	0	0	**1.0**	0	0	0	0	0	0	...	0
s_4	0	0	0	**1.0**	**1.0**	0	0	0	0	0	0	0	...	0
s_5	0	0	0	**1.0**	**1.0**	0	0	0	0	0	0	0	...	0
s_6	0	0	**1.0**	0	0	**1.0**	0	0	0	0	0	0	...	0
s_7	0	0	0	0	0	0	1.0	0	0	0	0	0	...	0
s_8	0	0	0	0	0	0	0	1.0	0	0	0	0	...	0
s_9	0	0	0	0	0	0	0	0	1.0	0	0	0	...	0
s_{10}	0	0	0	0	0	0	0	0	0	1.0	0	0	...	0
s_{11}	0	0	0	0	0	0	0	0	0	0	1.0	0	...	0

Table 6: The learned reward function for the learned dialogue MDP from SmartWheeler dialogues using keyword features.

6.2 Choice of features

IRL needs features to represent the reward function. We propose *keyword* features for applying IRL on the learned dialogue MDP/POMDP from SmartWheeler. The keyword features are automatically learned as the top-one words for each user intent (see Table 3). There are nine learned keywords:

forward, backward, right, left, turn, go, for, top, stop.

The keyword features for each state of SmartWheeler dialogue POMDP are represented in a vector, as shown in Table 5. The figure shows that states s_3, (*turn-right-little*) and s_6 (*follow-right-wall*) share the same features, i.e., *right*. Moreover, states s_4 (*turn-left-little*) and s_5 (*follow-left-wall*) share the same feature, i.e., *left*. In our experiments, we used *keyword-action-wise* feature representation. Such features include an indicator function for each pair of state-keyword and action. Thus, the feature size for SmartWheeler equals $216 = 9 \times 24$ (9 keywords and 24 actions).

Note that the choice of features is application dependent. The reason for using keywords as state features is that in the intent-based dialogue applications the states are the dialogue intents, where each intent is described as a vector of k-top words from the domain dialogues. Therefore, the keyword features are relevant features for the states.

7 Conclusion

In this paper, we described our our systematic approach for learning dialogue (PO)MDP model components from unannotated dialogues. In our approach, we start by learning the dialogue (PO)MDP states, i.e., the learned user intents from data. The learned states were then used for learning the user model. Building off these model components, we learned the agent's reward function by implementing a model-based IRL algorithm. We demonstrated our experiments on data collected in a healthcare domain to learn the dialogue model components solely from data.

8 Ongoing work

We are working on a variation of MDP-IRL algorithm, that is a model-free trajectory-based MDP-IRL algorithm. In the model-free MDPs, the states are usually presented using features (and thus there is no defined/learned transition model). Then, model-free MDP algorithms are used for estimating the optimal strategy of such MDPs. Model-free MDPs can be used in the place of POMDPs where state features are analogous to observations.

In this context, data analysis for feature selection is highly important. Dialogue features can be used to represent dialogue situations (as well as the observations in the dialogue POMDPs). Moreover, the IRL algorithms require (dialogue) features for representing the reward function. As mentioned earlier, the reward function of (PO)MDPs highly affects the optimized strategy. A relevant reward function to the dialogue agent and users can only be learned by studying and extracting relevant features from the dialogue domain. We would like to learn the relevant and proper features that are suitable for both state features as well as the reward representation. In particular, we are going to use the experts' (caregivers') strategies in the place of a (PO)MDP strategy in order to learn a reward function that accounts for caregivers' strategies.

9 Acknowledgment

The authors thank Jason D. Williams and Suhrid Balakrishnan for helpful discussions in the early development of this work. The authors also thank Joelle Pineau for providing them with the Smartwheeler data. The dataset has been collected with contributions from researchers at McGill University, École Polytechnique de Montréal, Université de Montréal, and the Centre de réadaptation Lucie-Bruneau and Constance-Lethbridge. The authors thank Ethan Selfridge for his help in proofreading. Last but not least, many thank to FQRNT (Fonds Québécois de la recherche sur la nature et les technologies) for partial financial support of this work.

References

David M. Blei, Andrew Y. Ng, and Michael I. Jordan. 2003. Latent Dirichlet allocation. *Journal of Machine Learning Research*, 3:993–1022.

Jennifer Boger, Pascal Poupart, Jesse Hoey, Craig Boutilier, Geoff Fernie, and Alex Mihailidis. 2005. A decision-theoretic approach to task assistance for persons with dementia. In *Proceedings of the 19th International Joint Conference on Artificial Intelligence (IJCAI'05)*, pages 1293–1299, San Francisco, CA, USA. Morgan Kaufmann Publishers Inc.

Milica Gašić. 2011. *Statistical Dialogue Modelling*. Ph.D. thesis, Department of Engineering, University of Cambridge.

Amit Gruber, Michal Rosen-Zvi, and Yair Weiss. 2007. Hidden topic Markov models. In *Artificial Intelligence and Statistics (AISTATS'07)*, San Juan, Puerto Rico, USA.

D. Kim, J. Kim, and K.E. Kim. 2011. Robust performance evaluation of POMDP-based dialogue systems. *IEEE Transactions on Audio, Speech, and Language Processing*, 19(4):1029–1040.

Andrew Y. Ng and Stuart J. Russell. 2000. Algorithms for inverse reinforcement learning. In *Proceedings of the 17th International Conference on Machine Learning (ICML'00), Stanford, CA, USA*.

T. Paek and R. Pieraccini. 2008. Automating spoken dialogue management design using machine learning: An industry perspective. *Speech Communication*, 50(8):716–729.

Joelle Pineau, Robert West, Amin Atrash, Julien Villemure, and Francois Routhier. 2011. On the feasibility of using a standardized test for evaluating a speech-controlled smart wheelchair. *International Journal of Intelligent Control and Systems*, 16(2):124–131.

Nicholas Roy, Joelle Pineau, and Sebastian Thrun. 2000. Spoken dialogue management using probabilistic reasoning. In *Proceedings of the 38th Annual Meeting on Association for Computational Linguistics (ACL'00), Hong Kong*.

Frank Rudzicz, Rozanne Wilson, Alex Mihailidis, Elizabeth Rochon, and Carol Leonard. 2012. Communication strategies for a computerized caregiver for individuals with alzheimer's disease. In *Proceedings of the Third Workshop on Speech and Language Processing for Assistive Technologies, (SLPAT'12)*, pages 47–55, Montreal, Quebec, Canada. Association for Computational Linguistics.

Blaise Thomson and Steve Young. 2010. Bayesian update of dialogue state: A POMDP framework for spoken dialogue systems. *Computer Speech and Language*, 24(4):562–588.

Jason D. Williams. 2006. *Partially Observable Markov Decision Processes for Spoken Dialogue Management*. Ph.D. thesis, Department of Engineering, University of Cambridge.

Bo Zhang, Qingsheng Cai, Jianfeng Mao, and Baining Guo. 2001. Planning and acting under uncertainty: A new model for spoken dialogue system. In *Proceedings of the 17th Conference in Uncertainty in Artificial Intelligence (UAI'01), Seattle, Washington, USA*, August.

Speech recognition in Alzheimer's disease with personal assistive robots

Frank Rudzicz[1,2,*] and **Rosalie Wang**[1] and **Momotaz Begum**[3] and **Alex Mihailidis**[2,1]
[1] Toronto Rehabilitation Institute, Toronto ON; [2] University of Toronto, Toronto ON;
[3] University of Massachussetts Lowell
*frank@cs.toronto.edu

Abstract

To help individuals with Alzheimer's disease live at home for longer, we are developing a mobile robotic platform, called ED, intended to be used as a personal caregiver to help with the performance of activities of daily living. In a series of experiments, we study speech-based interactions between each of 10 older adults with Alzheimers disease and ED as the former makes tea in a simulated home environment. Analysis reveals that speech recognition remains a challenge for this recording environment, with word-level accuracies between 5.8% and 19.2% during household tasks with individuals with Alzheimer's disease. This work provides a baseline assessment for the types of technical and communicative challenges that will need to be overcome in human-robot interaction for this population.

1 Introduction

Alzheimer's disease (AD) is a progressive neurodegenerative disorder primarily impairing memory, followed by declines in language, ability to carry out motor tasks, object recognition, and executive functioning (American Psychiatric Association, 2000; Gauthier et al., 1997). An accurate measure of functional decline comes from performance in activities of daily living (ADLs), such as shopping, finances, housework, and self-care tasks. The deterioration in language comprehension and/or production resulting from specific brain damage, also known as aphasia, is a common feature of AD and other related conditions. Language changes observed clinically in older adults with dementia include increasing word-finding difficulties, loss of ability to verbally express information in detail, increasing use of generic references (e.g., "it"), and progressing difficulties understanding information presented verbally (American Psychiatric Association, 2000).

Many nations are facing healthcare crises in the lack of capacity to support rapidly aging populations nor the chronic conditions associated with aging, including dementia. The current healthcare model of removing older adults from their homes and placing them into long-term care facilities is neither financially sustainable in this scenario (Bharucha et al., 2009), nor is it desirable. Our team has been developing "smart home" systems at the Toronto Rehabilitation Institute (TRI, part of the University Health Network) to help older adults "age-in-place" by providing different types of support, such as step-by-step prompts for daily tasks (Mihailidis et al., 2008), responses to emergency situations (Lee and Mihaildis, 2005), and means to communicate with family and friends. These systems are being evaluated within a completely functional re-creation of a one-bedroom apartment located within The TRI hospital, called HomeLab. These smart home technologies use advanced sensing techniques and machine learning to autonomously react to their users, but they are fixed and embedded into the environment, e.g., as cameras in the ceiling. Fixing the location of these technologies carries a tradeoff between utility and feasibility – installing multiple hardware units at all locations where assistance could be required (e.g., bathroom, kitchen, and bedroom) can be expensive and cumbersome, but installing too few units will present gaps where a user's activity will not be detected. Alternatively, integrating personal mobile robots with smart homes can overcome some of these tradeoffs. Moreover, assistance provided via a physically embodied robot is often more acceptable than that provided by an embedded system (Klemmer et al., 2006).

With these potential advantages in mind, we conducted a 'Wizard-of-Oz' study to explore the

Proceedings of the 5th Workshop on Speech and Language Processing for Assistive Technologies (SLPAT), pages 20–28,
Baltimore, Maryland USA, August 26 2014.

feasibility and usability of a mobile assistive robot that uses the step-by-step prompting approaches for daily activities originally applied to our smart home research (Mihailidis et al., 2008). We conducted the study with older adults with mild or moderate AD and the tasks of hand washing and tea making. Our preliminary data analysis showed that the participants reacted well to the robot itself and the prompts that it provided, suggesting the feasibility of using personal robots for this application (Begum et al., 2013). One important identified issue is the need for an automatic speech recognition system to detect and understand utterances specifically from older adults with AD. The development of such a system will enable the assistive robot to better understand the behaviours and needs of these users for effective interactions and will further enhance environmental-based smart home systems.

This paper presents an analysis of the speech data collected from our participants with AD when interacting with the robot. In a series of experiments, we measure the performance of modern speech recognition with this population and with their younger caregivers with and without signal preprocessing. This work will serve as the basis for further studies by identifying some of the development needs of a speech-based interface for robotic caregivers for older adults with AD.

2 Related Work

Research in smart home systems, assistive robots, and integrated robot/smart home systems for older adults with cognitive impairments has often focused on assistance with activities of daily living (i.e., reminders to do specific activities according to a schedule or prompts to perform activity steps), cognitive and social stimulation and emergency response systems. Archipel (Serna et al., 2007) recognizes the user's intended plan and provides prompts, e.g. with cooking tasks. Autominder, (Pollack, 2006), provides context-appropriate reminders for activity schedules, and the COACH (Cognitive Orthosis for Assisting with aCtivities in the Home) system prompts for the task of handwashing (Mihailidis et al., 2008) and tea-making (Olivier et al., 2009). Mynatt et al. (2004) have been developing technologies to support aging-in-place such as the Cooks Collage, which uses a series of photos to remind the user what the last step completed was if the user is interrupted during a cooking task. These interventions tend to be embedded in existing environments (e.g., around the sink area).

More recent innovations have examined integrated robot-smart home systems where systems are embedded into existing environments that communicate with mobile assistive robots (e.g., CompanionAble, (Mouad et al., 2010); Mobiserv Kompai, (Lucet, 2012); and ROBADOM (Tapus and Chetouani, 2010)). Many of these projects are targeted towards older adults with cognitive impairment, and not specifically those with significant cognitive impairment. One of these systems, CompanionAble, with a fully autonomous assistive robot, has recently been tested in a simulated home environment for two days each with four older adults with dementia (AD or Pick's disease/frontal lobe dementia) and two with mild cognitive impairment. The system provides assistance with various activities, including appointment reminders for activities input by users or caregivers, video calls, and cognitive exercises. Participants reported an overall acceptance of the system and several upgrades were reported, including a speech recognition system that had to be deactivated by the second day due to poor performance.

One critical component for the successful use of these technological interventions is the usability of the communication interface for the targeted users, in this case older adults with Alzheimer's disease. As in communication between two people, communication between the older adult and the robot may include natural, freeform speech (as opposed to simple spoken keyword interaction) and non-verbal cues (e.g., hand gestures, head pose, eye gaze, facial feature cues), although speech tends to be far more effective (Green et al., 2008; Goodrich and Schultz, 2007). Previous research indicates that automated communication systems are more effective if they take into account the affective and mental states of the user (Saini et al., 2005). Indeed, speech appears to be the most powerful mode of communication for an assistive robot to communicate with its users (Tapus and Chetouani, 2010; Lucet, 2012).

2.1 Language use in dementia and Alzheimer's disease

In order to design a speech interface for individuals with dementia, and AD in particular, it is important to understand how their speech differs from that of the general population. This then can be integrated into future automatic speech recognition systems. Guinn and Habash (2012) showed, through an analysis of conversational dialogs, that repetition, incomplete words, and paraphrasing were significant indicators of Alzheimer's disease relative but several expected measures such as filler phrases, syllables per minute, and pronoun rate were not. Indeed, pauses, fillers, formulaic speech, restarts, and speech disfluencies are all hallmarks of speech in individuals with Alzheimer's (Davis and Maclagan, 2009; Snover et al., 2004). Effects of Alzheimer's disease on syntax remains controversial, with some evidence that deficits in syntax or of agrammatism could be due to memory deficits in the disease (Reilly et al., 2011).

Other studies has applied similar analyses to related clinical groups. Pakhomov et al. (2010) identified several different features from the audio and corresponding transcripts of 38 patients with frontotemporal lobar degeneration (FTLD). They found that pause-to-word ratio and pronoun-to-noun ratios were especially discriminative of FTLD variants and that length, hesitancy, and agramatism correspond to the phenomenology of FTLD. Roark et al. (2011) tested the ability of an automated classifier to distinguish patients with mild cognitive impairment from healthy controls that include acoustic features such as pause frequency and duration.

2.2 Human-robot interaction

Receiving assistance from an entity with a physical body (such as a robot) is often psychologically more acceptable than receiving assistance from an entity without a physical body (such as an embedded system) (Klemmer et al., 2006). Physical embodiment also opens up the possibility of having more meaningful interaction between the older adult and the robot, as discussed in Section 5.

Social collaboration between humans and robots often depends on communication in which each participant's intention and goals are clear (Freedy et al., 2007; Bauer et al., 2008; Green et al., 2008). It is important that the human participant is able to construct a useable 'mental model' of the robot through bidirectional communication (Burke and Murphy, 1999) which can include both natural speech and non-verbal cues (e.g., hand gestures, gaze, facial cues), although speech tends to be far more effective (Green et al., 2008; Goodrich and Schultz, 2007).

Automated communicative systems that are more sensitive to the emotive and the mental states of their users are often more successful than more neutral conversational agents (Saini et al., 2005). In order to be useful in practice, these communicative systems need to mimic some of the techniques employed by caregivers of individuals with AD. Often, these caregivers are employed by local clinics or medical institutions and are trained by those institutions in ideal verbal *communication strategies* for use with those having dementia (Hopper, 2001; Goldfarb and Pietro, 2004). These include (Wilson et al., 2012) but are not limited to relatively slow rate of speech, verbatim repetition of misunderstood prompts, closed-ended (e.g., 'yes/no') questions, and reduced syntactic complexity. However, Tomoeda et al. (1990) showed that rates of speech that are too slow may interfere with comprehension if they introduce problems of short-term retention of working memory. Small et al. (1997) showed that paraphrased repetition is just as effective as verbatim repetition (indeed, syntactic variation of common semantics may assist comprehension). Furthermore, Rochon et al. (2000) suggested that the syntactic complexity of utterances is not necessarily the only predictor of comprehension in individuals with AD; rather, correct comprehension of the semantics of sentences is inversely related to the increasing number of propositions used – it is preferable to have as few clauses or core ideas as possible, i.e., one-at-a-time.

3 Data collection

The data in this paper come from a study to examine the feasibility and usability of a personal assistive robot to assist older adults with AD in the completion of daily activities (Begum et al., 2013). Ten older adults diagnosed with AD, aged ≥ 55, and their caregivers were recruited from a local memory clinic in Toronto, Canada. Ethics approval was received from the Toronto Rehabilitation Institute and the University of Toronto. Inclusion criteria included fluency in English, normal hearing, and difficulty completing common sequences of steps, according to their caregivers. Caregivers had to be a family or privately-hired caregiver who provides regular care (e.g., 7 hours/week) to the older adult participant. Following informed consent, the older adult participants were screened using the Mini Mental State Exam (MMSE) (Folstein et al., 2001) to ascertain their general level of cognitive impairment. Table 1 summarizes relevant demographics.

	Sex	Age (years)	MMSE (/30)
OA1	F	76	9
OA2	M	86	24
OA3	M	88	25
OA4	F	77	25
OA5	F	59	18
OA6	M	63	23
OA7	F	77	25
OA8	F	83	19
OA9	F	84	25
OA10	M	85	15

Table 1: Demographics of older adults (OA).

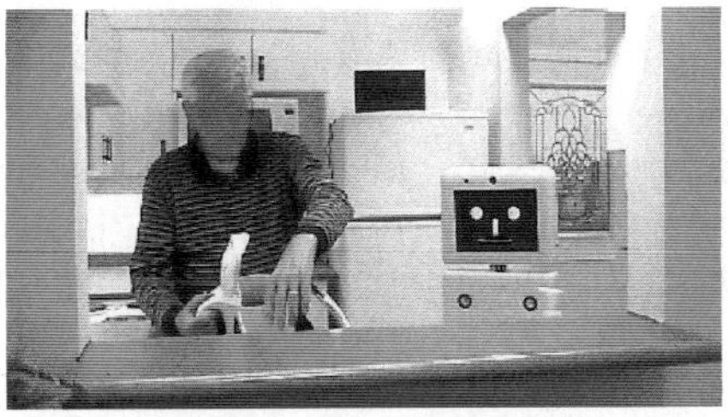

(a)

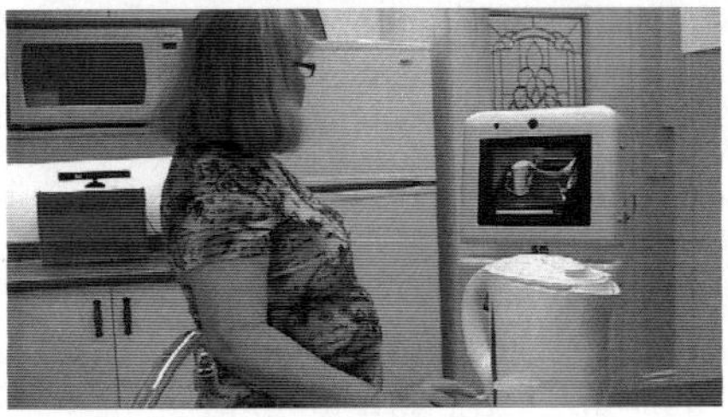

(b)

Figure 1: ED and two participants with AD during the tea-making task in the kitchen of HomeLab at TRI.

3.1 ED, the personal caregiver robot

The robot was built on an iRobot base (operating speed: 28 cm/second) and both its internal construction and external enclosure were designed and built at TRI. It is 102 cm in height and has separate body and head components; the latter is primarily a LCD monitor that shows audiovisual prompts or displays a simple 'smiley face' otherwise, as shown in Figure 2. The robot has two speakers embedded in its 'chest', two video cameras (one in the head and one near the floor, for navigation), and a microphone. For this study, the built-in microphones were not used in favor of environmental Kinect microphones, discussed below. This was done to account for situations when the robot and human participant were not in the same room simultaneously.

The robot was tele-operated throughout the task. The tele-operator continuously monitored the task progress and the overall affective state of the participants in a video stream sent by the robot and triggered social conversation, asked task-related questions, and delivered prompts to guide the participants towards successful completion of the tea-making task (Fig. 1).

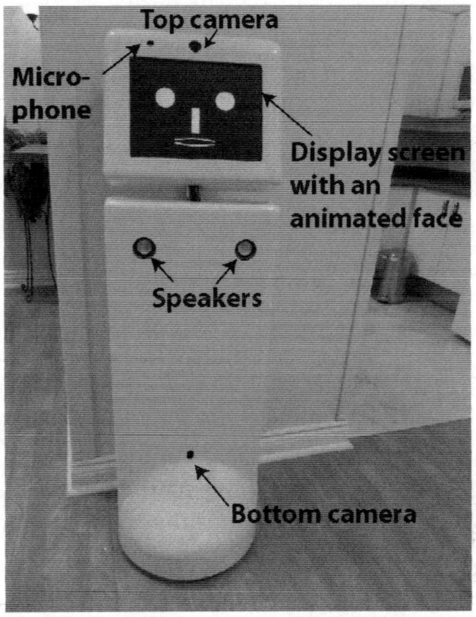

Figure 2: The prototype robotic caregiver, ED.

The robot used the Cepstral commercial text-to-speech (TTS) system using the U.S. English voice 'David' and its default parameters. This system is based on the Festival text-to-speech platform in many respects, including its use of linguistic preprocessing (e.g., part-of-speech tagging) and certain heuristics (e.g., letter-to-sound rules). Spoken prompts consisted of simple sentences, sometimes accompanied by short video demonstrations designed to be easy to follow by people with a cognitive impairment.

For efficient prompting, the tea-making task was broken down into different steps or sub-task. Audio or audio-video prompts corresponding to each of these sub-tasks were recorded prior to data collection. The human-robot interaction proceeded according to the following script when collaborating with the participants:

1. Allow the participant to initiate steps in each sub-task, if they wish.
2. If a participant asks for directions, deliver the appropriate prompt.
3. If a participant requests to perform the sub-task in their own manner, agree if this does not involve skipping an essential step.
4. If a participant asks about the location of an item specific to the task, provide a full-body gesture by physically orienting the robot towards the sought item.
5. During water boiling, ask the participant to put sugar or milk or tea bag in the cup. Time permitting, engage in a social conversation, e.g., about the weather.
6. When no prerecorded prompt sufficiently answers a participant question, respond with the correct answer (or *"I don't know"*) through the TTS engine.

3.2 Study set-up and procedures

Consent included recording video, audio, and depth images with the Microsoft Kinect sensor in HomeLab for all interviews and interactions with ED. Following informed consent, older adults and their caregivers were interviewed to acquire background information regarding their daily activities, the set-up of their home environment, and the types of assistance that the caregiver typically provided for the older adult.

Participants were asked to observe ED moving in HomeLab and older adult participants were asked to have a brief conversation with ED to become oriented with the robot's movement and speech characteristics. The older adults were then asked to complete the hand-washing and tea-making tasks in the bathroom and kitchen, respectively, with ED guiding them to the locations and providing specific step-by-step prompts, as necessary. The tele-operator observed the progress of the task, and delivered the pre-recorded prompts corresponding to the task step to guide the older adult to complete each task. The TTS system was used to respond to task-related questions and to engage in social conversation. The caregivers were asked to observe the two tasks and to intervene only if necessary (e.g., if the older adult showed signs of distress or discomfort). The older adult and caregiver participants were then interviewed separately to gain their feedback on the feasibility of using such a robot for assistance with daily activities and usability of the system. Each study session lasted approximately 2.5 hours including consent, introduction to the robot, tea-making interaction with the robot, and post-interaction interviews. The average duration for the tea-making task alone was 12 minutes.

4 Experiments and analysis

Automatic speech recognition given these data is complicated by several factors, including a preponderance of utterances in which human caregivers speak concurrently with the participants, as well as inordinately challenging levels of noise. The estimated signal-to-noise ratio (SNR) across utterances range from -3.42 dB to 8.14 dB, which is extremely low compared to typical SNR of 40 dB in clean speech. One cause of this low SNR is that microphones are placed in the environment, rather than on the robot (so the distance to the microphone is variable, but relatively large) and that the participant often has their back turned to the microphone, as shown in figure 1.

As in previous work (Rudzicz et al., 2012), we enhance speech signals with the log-spectral amplitude estimator (LSAE) which minimizes the mean squared error of the log spectra given a model for the source speech $X_k = A_k e^{(j\omega_k)}$, where A_k is the spectral amplitude. The LSAE method is a modification of the short-time spectral amplitude estimator that finds an estimate of the spectral amplitude, $\hat{A}_k$, that minimizes the distortion

$$E\left[\left(logA_k - \log \hat{A}_k\right)^2\right], \tag{1}$$

such that the log-spectral amplitude estimate is

$$\begin{aligned}\hat{A}_k &= \exp\left(E\left[\ln A_k \mid Y_k\right]\right)\\ &= \frac{\xi_k}{1+\xi_k}\exp\left(\frac{1}{2}\int_{v_k}^{\infty}\frac{e^{-t}}{t}dt\right)R_k,\end{aligned} \tag{2}$$

where ξ_k is the *a priori* SNR, R_k is the noisy spectral amplitude, $v_k = \frac{\xi_k}{1+\xi_k}\gamma_k$, and γ_k is the *a posteriori* SNR (Erkelens et al., 2007). Often this is based on a Gaussian model of noise, as it is here (Ephraim and Malah, 1985).

As mentioned, there are many utterances in which human caregivers speak concurrently with the participants. This is partially confounded by the fact that utterances by individuals with AD tend to be shorter, so more of their utterance is lost, proportionally. Examples of this type where the caregiver's voice is louder than the participant's voice are discarded, amounting to about 10% of all utterances. In the following analyses, function words (i.e., prepositions, subordinating conjunctions, and determiners) are removed from consideration, although interjections are kept. Proper names are also omitted.

We use the HTK (Young et al., 2006) toolchain, which provides an implementation of a semi-continuous hidden Markov model (HMM) that allows state-tying and represents output densities by mixtures of Gaussians. Features consisted of the first 13 Mel-frequency cepstral coefficients, their first (δ) and second ($\delta\delta$) derivatives, and the log energy component, for 42 dimensions. Our own data were z-scaled regardless of whether LSAE noise reduction was applied.

Two language models (LMs) are used, both trigram models derived from the English Gigaword corpus, which contains 1200 word tokens (Graff and Cieri, 2003). The first LM uses the first 5000 most frequent words and the second uses the first 64,000 most frequent words of that corpus. Five acoustic models (AMs) are used with 1, 2, 4, 8, and 16 Gaussians per output density respectively. These are trained with approximately 211 hours of spoken transcripts of the *Wall Street Journal* (WSJ) from over one hundred non-pathological speakers (Vertanen, 2006).

Table 2 shows, for the small- and large-vocabulary LMs, the word-level accuracies of the baseline HTK ASR system, as determined by the inverse of the Levenshtein edit distance, for two scenarios (sit-down interviews vs. during the task), with and without LSAE noise reduction, for speech from individuals with AD and for their caregivers. These values are computed over all complexities of acoustic model and are consistent with other tasks of this type (i.e., with the challenges associated with the population and recording set up), with this type of relatively unconstrained ASR (Rudzicz et al., 2012). Applying LSAE results in a significant increase in accuracy for both the small-vocabulary (right-tailed homoscedastic $t(58) = 3.9, p < 0.005, CI = [6.19, \infty]$) and large-vocabulary (right-tailed homoscedastic $t(58) = 2.4, p < 0.01, CI = [2.58, \infty]$) tasks. For the participants with AD, ASR accuracy is significantly higher in interviews (paired $t(39) = 8.7, p < 0.0001, CI = [13.8, \infty]$), which is expected due in large part to the closer proximity of the microphone. Surprisingly, ASR accuracy on participants with ASR was not significantly different than on caregivers (two-tailed heteroscedastic $t(78) = -0.32, p = 0.75, CI = [-5.54, 4.0]$).

Figure 3 shows the mean ASR accuracy, with standard error ($\sigma/\sqrt{n}$), for each of the small-vocabulary and large-vocabulary ASR systems. The exponential function $b_0 + b_1 \exp(b_2 x)$ is fit to these data for each set, where b_i are coefficients that are iteratively adjustable via mean squared error. For the small-vocabulary data, $R^2 = 0.277$ and $F_8 = 3.06, p = 0.12$ versus the constant model. For the large-vocabulary data, $R^2 = 0.445$ and $F_8 = 2.81, p = 0.13$ versus the constant model. Clearly, there is an increasing trend in ASR accuracy with MMSE scores, however an n-way ANOVA on ASR accuracy scores reveals that this increase is not significant ($F_1 = 47.07, p = 0.164$). Furthermore, neither the age ($F_1 = 1.39, p = 0.247$) nor the sex ($F_1 = 0.98, p = 0.33$) of the participant had a significant effect on ASR accuracy. An additional n-way ANOVA reveals no strong interaction effects between age, sex, and MMSE.

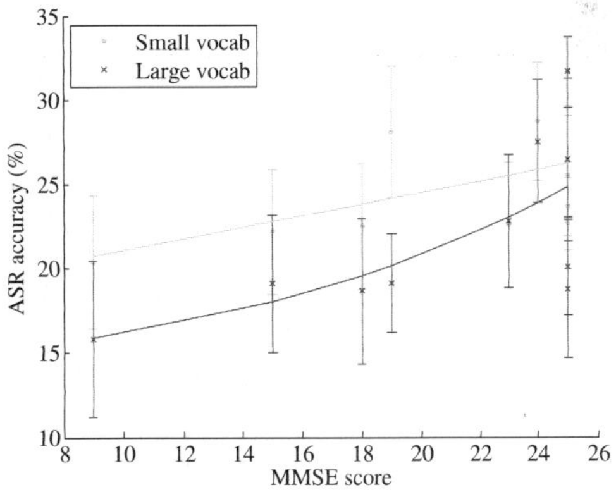

Figure 3: MMSE score versus mean ASR accuracy (with std. error bars) and fits of exponential regression for each of the small-vocabulary and large-vocabulary ASR systems.

	Scenario	Noise reduction	AD	caregiver
Small vocabulary	Interview	None	25.1 ($\sigma = 9.9$)	28.8 ($\sigma = 6.0$)
		LSAE	40.9 ($\sigma = 5.6$)	40.2 ($\sigma = 5.3$)
	In task	None	13.7 ($\sigma = 3.7$)	-
		LSAE	19.2 ($\sigma = 9.8$)	-
Large vocabulary	Interview	None	23.7 ($\sigma = 12.9$)	27.0 ($\sigma = 10.0$)
		LSAE	38.2 ($\sigma = 6.3$)	35.1 ($\sigma = 11.2$)
	In task	None	5.8 ($\sigma = 3.7$)	-
		LSAE	14.3 ($\sigma = 12.8$)	-

Table 2: ASR accuracy (means, and std. dev.) across speakers, scenario (interviews vs. during the task), and presence of noise reduction for the small and large language models.

5 Discussion

This study examined low-level aspects of speech recognition among older adults with Alzheimer's disease interacting with a robot in a simulated home environment. The best word-level accuracies of 40.9% ($\sigma = 5.6$) and 39.2% ($\sigma = 6.3$) achievable with noise reduction and in a quiet interview setting are comparable with the state-of-the-art in unrestricted large-vocabulary text entry. These results form the basis for ongoing work in ASR and interaction design for this domain. The trigram language model used in this work encapsulates the statistics of a large amount of speech from the general population – it is a speaker-independent model derived from a combination of English news agencies that is not necessarily representative of the type of language used in the home, or by our target population. The acoustic models were also derived from newswire data read by younger adults in quiet environments. We are currently training and adapting language models tuned specifically to older adults with Alzheimer's disease using data from the Carolina Conversations database (Pope and Davis, 2011) and the DementiaBank database (Boller and Becker, 1983).

Additionally, to function realistically, a lot of ambient and background noise will need to be overcome. We are currently looking into deploying a sensor network in the HomeLab that will include microphone arrays. Another method of improving rates of correct word recognition is to augment the process from redundant information from a concurrent sensory stream, i.e., in multimodal interaction (Rudzicz, 2006). Combining gesture and eye gaze with speech, for example, can be used to disambiguate speech-only signals.

Although a focus of this paper, verbal information is not the only modality in which human-robot interaction can take place. Indeed, Wilson et al. (2012) showed that experienced human caregivers employed various non-verbal and semi-verbal strategies to assist older adults with dementia about $1/3$ as often as verbal strategies (see section 2.2). These non-verbal and semi-verbal strategies included eye contact, sitting face-to-face, using hand gestures, a calm tone of voice, instrumental touch, exaggerated facial expressions, and moving slowly. Multi-modal communication can be extremely important for individuals with dementia, who may require redundant channels for disambiguating communication problems, especially if they have a language impairment or a significant hearing impairment.

It is vital that our current technological approaches to caring for the elderly in their homes progresses quickly, given the demographic shift in many nations worldwide. This paper provides a baseline assessment for the types of technical and communicative challenges that will need to be overcome in the near future to provide caregiving assistance to a growing number of older adults.

6 Acknowledgements

The authors would like to thank Rajibul Huq and Colin Harry, who designed and built the robot, Jennifer Boger and Goldie Nejat for their assistance in designing the study, and Sharon Cohen for her consultations during the study.

References

American Psychiatric Association. 2000. Delirium, dementia, and amnestic and other cognitive disorders. In *Diagnostic and Statistical Manual of Mental Disorders, Text Revision (DSM-IV-TR)*, chapter 2. American Psychiatric Association, Arlington, VA, fourth edition.

A. Bauer, D. Wollherr, and M. Buss. 2008. Human-robot collaboration: A survey. *International Journal of Humanoid Robotics*, 5:47–66.

Momotaz Begum, Rosalie Wang, Rajibul Huq, and Alex Mihailidis. 2013. Performance of daily activities by older adults with dementia: The role of an assistive robot. In *Proceedings of the IEEE International Conference on Rehabilitation Robotics*, Washington USA, June.

Ashok J. Bharucha, Vivek Anand, Jodi Forlizzi, Mary Amanda Dew, Charles F. Reynolds III, Scott Stevens, and Howard Wactlar. 2009. Intelligent assistive technology applications to dementia care: Current capabilities, limitations, and future challenges. *American Journal of Geriatric Psychiatry*, 17(2):88–104, February.

François Boller and James Becker. 1983. DementiaBank database.

J.L. Burke and R.R. Murphy. 1999. Situation awareness, team communication, and task performance in robot-assisted technical search: Bujold goes to bridgeport. CMPSCI Tech. Rep. CRASAR-TR2004-23, University of South Florida.

B. Davis and M. Maclagan. 2009. Examining pauses in Alzheimer's discourse. *American journal of Alzheimer's Disease and other dementias*, 24(2):141–154.

Y. Ephraim and D. Malah. 1985. Speech enhancement using a minimum mean-square error log-spectral amplitude estimator. *Acoustics, Speech and Signal Processing, IEEE Transactions on*, 33(2):443 – 445, apr.

Jan Erkelens, Jesper Jensen, and Richard Heusdens. 2007. A data-driven approach to optimizing spectral speech enhancement methods for various error criteria. *Speech Communication*, 49:530–541.

M. F. Folstein, S. E. Folstein, T. White, and M. A. Messer. 2001. *Mini-Mental State Examination user's guide*. Odessa (FL): Psychological Assessment Resources.

A. Freedy, E. de Visser, G. Weltman, and N. Coeyman. 2007. Measurement of trust in human-robot collaboration. In *Proceedings of International Conference on Collaborative Technologies and Systems*, pages 17 –24.

Serge Gauthier, Michel Panisset, Josephine Nalbantoglu, and Judes Poirier. 1997. Alzheimer's disease: current knowledge, management and research. *Canadian Medical Association Journal*, 157:1047–1052.

R. Goldfarb and M.J.S. Pietro. 2004. Support systems: Older adults with neurogenic communication disorders. *Journal of Ambulatory Care Management*, 27(4):356–365.

M. A. Goodrich and A. C. Schultz. 2007. Human-robot interaction: A survey. *Foundations and Trends in Human-Computer Interaction*, 1:203–275.

David Graff and Christopher Cieri. 2003. English gigaword. Linguistic Data Consortium.

S. A. Green, M. Billinghurst, X. Chen, and J. G. Chase. 2008. Human-robot collaboration: A literature review and augmented reality approach in design. *International Journal Advanced Robotic Systems*, 5:1–18.

Curry Guinn and Anthony Habash. 2012. Technical Report FS-12-01, Association for the Advancement of Artificial Intelligence.

T Hopper. 2001. Indirect interventions to facilitate communication in Alzheimers disease. *Seminars in Speech and Language*, 22(4):305–315.

S. Klemmer, B. Hartmann, and L. Takayama. 2006. How bodies matter: five themes for interaction design. In *Proceedings of the conference on Designing Interactive systems*, pages 140–149.

Tracy Lee and Alex Mihaildis. 2005. An intelligent emergency response system: Preliminary development and testing of automated fall detection. *Journal of Telemedicine and Telecare*, 11:194–198.

Eric Lucet. 2012. Social Mobiserv Kompai Robot to Assist People. In *euRobotics workshop on Robots in Healthcare and Welfare*.

Alex Mihailidis, Jennifer N Boger, Tammy Craig, and Jesse Hoey. 2008. The COACH prompting system to assist older adults with dementia through handwashing: An efficacy study. *BMC Geriatrics*, 8(28).

Mehdi Mouad, Lounis Adouane, Pierre Schmitt, Djamel Khadraoui, Benjamin Gâteau, and Philippe Martinet. 2010. Multi-agents based system to coordinate mobile teamworking robots. In *Proceedings of the 4th Companion Robotics Institute*, Brussels.

Elizabeth D. Mynatt, Anne-Sophie Melenhorst, Arthur D. Fisk, and Wendy A. Rogers. 2004. Aware technologies for aging in place: Understanding user needs and attitudes. *IEEE Pervasive Computing*, 3:36–41.

Patrick Olivier, Andrew Monk, Guangyou Xu, and Jesse Hoey. 2009. Ambient kitchen: Designing situation services using a high fidelity prototyping environment. In *Proceedings of the ACM 2nd International Conference on Pervasive Technologies Related to Assistive Environments*, Corfu Greece.

S. V. Pakhomov, G. E. Smith, D. Chacon, Y. Feliciano, N. Graff-Radford, R. Caselli, and D. S. Knopman. 2010. Computerized analysis of speech and language to identify psycholinguistic correlates of frontotemporal lobar degeneration. *Cognitive and Behavioral Neurology*, 23:165–177.

M. E. Pollack. 2006. Autominder: A case study of assistive technology for elders with cognitive impairment. *Generations*, 30:67–69.

Charlene Pope and Boyd H. Davis. 2011. Finding a balance: The Carolinas Conversation Collection. *Corpus Linguistics and Linguistic Theory*, 7(1).

J. Reilly, J. Troche, and M. Grossman. 2011. Language processing in dementia. In A. E. Budson and N. W. Kowall, editors, *The Handbook of Alzheimer's Disease and Other Dementias*. Wiley-Blackwell.

Brian Roark, Margaret Mitchell, John-Paul Hosom, Kristy Hollingshead, and Jeffery Kaye. 2011. Spoken language derived measures for detecting mild cognitive impairment. *IEEE Transactions on Audio, Speech, and Language Processing*, 19(7):2081–2090.

Elizabeth Rochon, Gloria S. Waters, and David Caplan. 2000. The Relationship Between Measures of Working Memory and Sentence Comprehension in Patients With Alzheimer's Disease. *Journal of Speech, Language, and Hearing Research*, 43:395–413.

Frank Rudzicz, Rozanne Wilson, Alex Mihailidis, Elizabeth Rochon, and Carol Leonard. 2012. Communication strategies for a computerized caregiver for individuals with alzheimer's disease. In *Proceedings of the Third Workshop on Speech and Language Processing for Assistive Technologies (SLPAT2012) at the 13th Annual Conference of the North American Chapter of the Association for Computational Linguistics (NAACL 2012)*, Montreal Canada, June.

Frank Rudzicz. 2006. Clavius: Bi-directional parsing for generic multimodal interaction. In *Proceedings of the joint meeting of the International Conference on Computational Linguistics and the Association for Computational Linguistics*, Sydney Australia.

Privender Saini, Boris de Ruyter, Panos Markopoulos, and Albert van Breemen. 2005. Benefits of social intelligence in home dialogue systems. In *Proceedings of INTERACT 2005*, pages 510–521.

A. Serna, H. Pigot, and V. Rialle. 2007. Modeling the progression of alzheimer's disease for cognitive assistance in smart homes. *User Modelling and User-Adapted Interaction*, 17:415–438.

Jeff A. Small, Elaine S. Andersen, and Daniel Kempler. 1997. Effects of working memory capacity on understanding rate-altered speech. *Aging, Neuropsychology, and Cognition*, 4(2):126–139.

M. Snover, B. Dorr, and R. Schwartz. 2004. A lexically-driven algorithm for disfluency detection. In *'Proceedings of HLT-NAACL 2004: Short Papers*, pages 157–160.

Adriana Tapus and Mohamed Chetouani. 2010. ROBADOM: the impact of a domestic robot on the psychological and cognitive state of the elderly with mild cognitive impairment. In *Proceedings of the International Symposium on Quality of Life Technology Intelligent Systems for Better Living*, Las Vegas USA, June.

Cheryl K. Tomoeda, Kathryn A. Bayles, Daniel R. Boone, Alfred W. Kaszniak, and Thomas J. Slauson. 1990. Speech rate and syntactic complexity effects on the auditory comprehension of alzheimer patients. *Journal of Communication Disorders*, 23(2):151 – 161.

Keith Vertanen. 2006. Baseline WSJ acoustic models for HTK and Sphinx: Training recipes and recognition experiments. Technical report, Cavendish Laboratory, University of Cambridge.

Rozanne Wilson, Elizabeth Rochon, Alex Mihailidis, and Carol Leonard. 2012. Examining success of communication strategies used by formal caregivers assisting individuals with alzheimer's disease during an activity of daily living. *Journal of Speech, Language, and Hearing Research*, 55:328–341, April.

Steve Young, Gunnar Evermann, Mark Gales, Thomas Hain, Dan Kershaw, Xunying (Andrew) Liu, Gareth Moore, Julian Odell, Dave Ollason and Dan Povey, Valtcho Valtchev, and Phil Woodland. 2006. The HTK Book (version 3.4).

Individuality-preserving Voice Conversion for Articulation Disorders Using Dictionary Selective Non-negative Matrix Factorization

Ryo Aihara, Tetsuya Takiguchi, Yasuo Ariki
Graduate School of System Informatics, Kobe University
1-1, Rokkodai, Nada, Kobe, 6578501, Japan
aihara@me.cs.scitec.kobe-u.ac.jp,
takigu@kobe-u.ac.jp,
ariki@kobe-u.ac.jp

Abstract

We present in this paper a voice conversion (VC) method for a person with an articulation disorder resulting from athetoid cerebral palsy. The movements of such speakers are limited by their athetoid symptoms, and their consonants are often unstable or unclear, which makes it difficult for them to communicate. In this paper, exemplar-based spectral conversion using Non-negative Matrix Factorization (NMF) is applied to a voice with an articulation disorder. In order to preserve the speaker's individuality, we use a combined dictionary that was constructed from the source speaker's vowels and target speaker's consonants. However, this exemplar-based approach needs to hold all the training exemplars (frames), and it may cause mismatching of phonemes between input signals and selected exemplars. In this paper, in order to reduce the mismatching of phoneme alignment, we propose a phoneme-categorized sub-dictionary and a dictionary selection method using NMF. The effectiveness of this method was confirmed by comparing its effectiveness with that of a conventional Gaussian Mixture Model (GMM)-based and conventional NMF-based method.

1 Introduction

In this study, we focused on a person with an articulation disorder resulting from the athetoid type of cerebral palsy. About two babies in 1,000 are born with cerebral palsy (Hollegaard et al., 2013). Cerebral palsy results from damage to the central nervous system, and the damage causes movement disorders. Cerebral palsy is classified into the following types: 1)spastic, 2)athetoid, 3)ataxic, 4)atonic, 5)rigid, and a mixture of these types (Canale and Campbell, 2002).

Athetoid symptoms develop in about 10-15% of cerebral palsy sufferers (Hollegaard et al., 2013). In the case of a person with this type of articulation disorder, his/her movements are sometimes more unstable than usual. That means their utterances (especially their consonants) are often unstable or unclear due to the athetoid symptoms. Athetoid symptoms also restrict the movement of their arms and legs. Most people suffering from athetoid cerebral palsy cannot communicate by sign language or writing, so there is great need for voice systems for them.

In this paper, we propose a voice conversion (VC) method for articulation disorders. Regarding speech recognition for articulation disorders, the recognition rate using a speaker-independent model which is trained by well-ordered speech, is 3.5% (Matsumasa et al., 2009). This result implies that the utterance of a person with an articulation disorder is difficult to understand for people who have not communicated with them before. In recent years, people with an articulation disorder may use slideshows and a previously synthesized voice when they give a lecture. However, because their movement is restricted by their athetoid symptoms, to make slides or synthesize their voice in advance is hard for them. People with articulation disorders desire a VC system that converts their voice into a clear voice that preserves their voice's individuality. Rudzicz et al. (Rudzicz, 2011; Rudzicz, 2014) proposed speech adjustment method for people with articulation disorders based on the observations from the database.

In (Aihara et al., 2014), we proposed individuality-preserving VC for articulation disorders. In our VC, source exemplars and target exemplars are extracted from the parallel

Proceedings of the 5th Workshop on Speech and Language Processing for Assistive Technologies (SLPAT), pages 29–37,
Baltimore, Maryland USA, August 26 2014.

training data, having the same texts uttered by the source and target speakers. The input source signal is expressed with a sparse representation of the source exemplars using Non-negative Matrix Factorization (NMF). By replacing a source speaker's exemplar with a target speaker's exemplar, the original speech spectrum is replaced with the target speaker's spectrum. People with articulation disorders wish to communicate by their own voice if they can; therefore, we proposed a combined-dictionary, which consists of a source speaker's vowels and target speaker's well-ordered consonants. In the voice of a person with an articulation disorder, their consonants are often unstable and that makes their voices unclear. Their vowels are relatively stable compared to their consonants. Hence, by replacing the articulation-disordered basis of consonants only, a voice with an articulation disorder is converted into a non-disordered voice that preserves the individuality of the speaker's voice.

In this paper, we propose advanced individuality-preserving VC using NMF. In order to avoid a mixture of the source and target spectra in a converted phoneme, we applied a phoneme-categorized dictionary and a dictionary selection method to our VC using NMF. In conventional NMF-based VC, the number of dictionary frames becomes large because the dictionary holds all the training exemplar frames. Therefore, it may cause phoneme mismatching between input signals and selected exemplars and some frames of converted spectra might be mixed with the source and target spectra. In this paper, a training exemplar is divided into a phoneme-categorized sub-dictionary, and an input signal is converted by using the selected sub-dictionary. The effectiveness of this method was confirmed by comparing it with a conventional NMF-based method and a conventional Gaussian Mixture Model (GMM)-based method.

The rest of this paper is organized as follows: In Section 2, related works are introduced. In Section 3, the basic idea of NMF-based VC is described. In Section 4, our proposed method is described. In Section 5, the experimental data are evaluated, and the final section is devoted to our conclusions.

2 Related Works

Voice conversion (VC) is a technique for converting specific information in speech while maintaining the other information in the utterance. One of the most popular VC applications is speaker conversion (Stylianou et al., 1998). In speaker conversion, a source speaker's voice individuality is changed to a specified target speaker's so that the input utterance sounds as though a specified target speaker had spoken it.

There have also been studies on several tasks that make use of VC. Emotion conversion is a technique for changing emotional information in input speech while maintaining linguistic information and speaker individuality (Veaux and Robet, 2011). In recent years, VC has been used for automatic speech recognition (ASR) or speaker adaptation in text-to-speech (TTS) systems (Kain and Macon, 1998). These studies show the varied uses of VC.

Many statistical approaches to VC have been studied (Valbret et al., 1992). Among these approaches, the Gaussian mixture model (GMM)-based mapping approach (Stylianou et al., 1998) is widely used. In this approach, the conversion function is interpreted as the expectation value of the target spectral envelope. The conversion parameters are evaluated using Minimum Mean-Square Error (MMSE) on a parallel training set. A number of improvements in this approach have been proposed. Toda et al. (Toda et al., 2007) introduced dynamic features and the global variance (GV) of the converted spectra over a time sequence. Helander et al. (Helander et al., 2010) proposed transforms based on partial least squares (PLS) in order to prevent the over-fitting problem associated with standard multivariate regression. There have also been approaches that do not require parallel data that make use of GMM adaptation techniques (Lee and Wu, 2006) or eigen-voice GMM (EV-GMM) (Toda et al., 2006).

In the field of assistive technology, Nakamura et al. (Nakamura et al., 2012; Nakamura et al., 2006) proposed GMM-based VC systems that reconstruct a speaker's individuality in electrolaryngeal speech and speech recorded by NAM microphones. These systems are effective for electrolaryngeal speech and speech recorded by NAM microphones however, because these statistical approaches are mainly proposed for speaker conversion, the target speaker's individuality will be changed to the source speaker's individuality. People with articulation disorders wish to communicate by their own voice if they can and there is a needs for individuality-preserving VC.

Text-to-speech synthesis (TTS) is a famous voice application that is widely researched. Veaux et al. (Veaux et al., 2012) used HMM-based speech synthesis to reconstruct the voice of individuals with degenerative speech disorders resulting from Amyotrophic Lateral Sclerosis (ALS). Yamagishi et al. (Yamagishi et al., 2013) proposed a project named "Voice Banking and Reconstruction". In that project, various types of voices are collected and they proposed TTS for ALS using that database. The difference between TTS and VC is that TTS needs text input to synthesize speech, whereas VC does not need text input. In the case of people with articulation disorders resulting from athetoid cerebral palsy, it is difficult for them to input text because of their athetoid symptoms.

Our proposed NMF-based VC (Takashima et al., 2012) is an exemplar-based method using sparse representation, which is different from the conventional statistical method. In recent years, approaches based on sparse representations have gained interest in a broad range of signal processing. In approaches based on sparse representations, the observed signal is represented by a linear combination of a small number of bases. In some approaches for source separation, the atoms are grouped for each source, and the mixed signals are expressed with a sparse representation of these atoms. By using only the weights of the atoms related to the target signal, the target signal can be reconstructed. Gemmeke et al. (Gemmeke et al., 2011) also propose an exemplar-based method for noise-robust speech recognition. In that method, the observed speech is decomposed into the speech atoms, noise atoms, and their weights. Then the weights of the speech atoms are used as phonetic scores (instead of the likelihoods of hidden Markov models) for speech recognition.

In (Takashima et al., 2012), we proposed noise-robust VC using NMF. The noise exemplars, which are extracted from the before- and after-utterance sections in an observed signal, are used as the noise-dictionary, and the VC process is combined with an NMF-based noise-reduction method. On the other hand, NMF is one of the clustering methods. In our exemplar-based VC, if the phoneme label of the source exemplar is given, we can discriminate the phoneme of the input signal by using NMF. In this paper, we proposed a dictionary selection method using this property of NMF.

3 Voice Conversion Based on Non-negative Matrix Factorization

3.1 Basic Idea

In the exemplar-based approach, the observed signal is represented by a linear combination of a small number of bases.

$$\mathbf{x}_l \approx \sum_{j=1}^{J} \mathbf{a}_j h_{j,l} = \mathbf{A}\mathbf{h}_l \qquad (1)$$

$\mathbf{x}_l$ represents the l-th frame of the observation. $\mathbf{a}_j$ and $h_{j,l}$ represent the j-th basis and the weight, respectively. $\mathbf{A} = [\mathbf{a}_1 \ldots \mathbf{a}_J]$ and $\mathbf{h}_l = [h_{1,l} \ldots h_{J,l}]^T$ are the collection of the bases and the stack of weights. In this paper, each basis denotes the exemplar of the spectrum, and the collection of exemplar $\mathbf{A}$ and the weight vector $\mathbf{h}_l$ are called the 'dictionary' and 'activity', respectively. When the weight vector $\mathbf{h}_l$ is sparse, the observed signal can be represented by a linear combination of a small number of bases that have non-zero weights. Eq. (1) is expressed as the inner product of two matrices using the collection of the frames or bases.

$$\mathbf{X} \approx \mathbf{A}\mathbf{H} \qquad (2)$$

$$\mathbf{X} = [\mathbf{x}_1, \ldots, \mathbf{x}_L], \quad \mathbf{H} = [\mathbf{h}_1, \ldots, \mathbf{h}_L]. \qquad (3)$$

L represents the number of the frames.

Fig. 1 shows the basic approach of our exemplar-based VC, where D, L, and J represent the numbers of dimensions, frames, and bases, respectively. Our VC method needs two dictionaries that are phonemically parallel. $\mathbf{A}^s$ represents a source dictionary that consists of the source speaker's exemplars and $\mathbf{A}^t$ represents a target dictionary that consists of the target speaker's exemplars. These two dictionaries consist of the same words and are aligned with dynamic time warping (DTW) just as conventional GMM-based VC is. Hence, these dictionaries have the same number of bases.

This method assumes that when the source signal and the target signal (which are the same words but spoken by different speakers) are expressed with sparse representations of the source dictionary and the target dictionary, respectively, the obtained activity matrices are approximately equivalent. Fig. 2 shows an example of the activity matrices estimated from a Japanese word "ikioi" ("vigor" in English), where one is uttered by a male, the other is uttered by a female, and each dictionary is structured from just one word "ikioi" as the simple example.

As shown in Fig. 2, these activities have high energies at similar elements. For this reason, we assume that when there are parallel dictionaries, the activity of the source features estimated with the source dictionary may be able to be substituted with that of the target features. Therefore, the target speech can be constructed using the target dictionary and the activity of the source signal as shown in Fig. 1. In this paper, we use Non-negative Matrix Factorization (NMF), which is a sparse coding method in order to estimate the activity matrix.

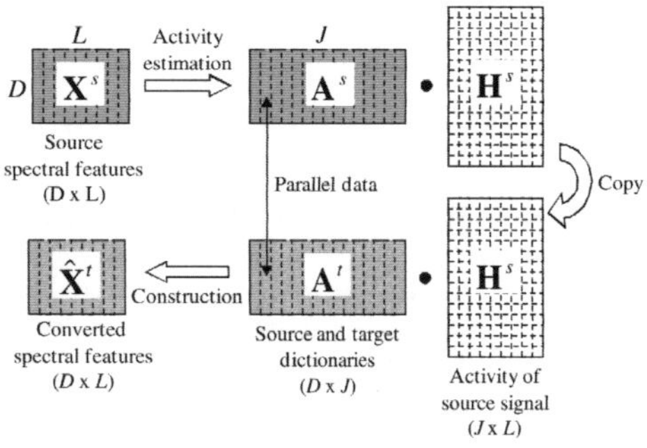

Figure 1: Basic approach of NMF-based voice conversion

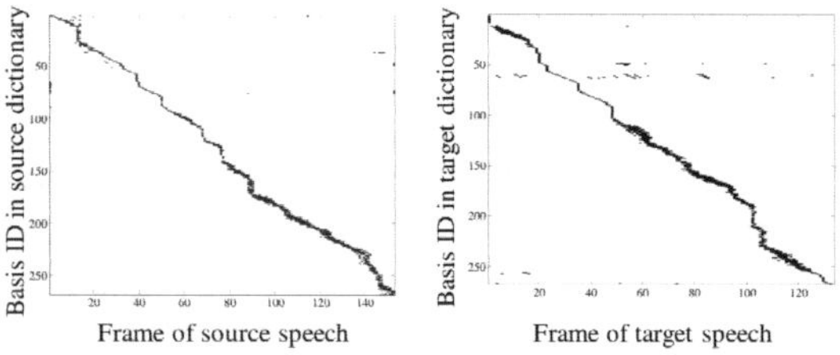

Figure 2: Activity matrices for parallel utterances

3.2 Individuality-preserving Voice Conversion Using Combined Dictionary

In order to make a parallel dictionary, some pairs of parallel utterances are needed, where each pair consists of the same text. One is spoken by a person with an articulation disorder (source speaker), and the other is spoken by a physically unimpaired person (target speaker). Spectrum envelopes, which are extracted from parallel utterances, are phonemically aligned by using DTW. In order to estimate activities of source features precisely, segment features, which consist of some consecutive frames, are constructed. Target features are constructed from consonant frames of the target's aligned spectrum and vowel frames of the source's aligned spectrum. Source and target dictionaries are constructed by lining up each of the features extracted from parallel utterances.

The vowels voiced by a speaker strongly indicate the speaker's individuality. On the other hand, consonants of people with articulation disorders are often unstable. Fig. 3(a) shows an example of the spectrogram for the word "ikioi" ("vigor" in English) of a person with an articulation disorder. The spectrogram of a physically unimpaired person speaking the same word is shown in Fig. 3(b). In Fig. 3(a), the area labeled "k" is not clear, compared to the same region in to Fig. 3(b). These figures indicate that consonants of people with articulation disorders are often unstable and this deteriorates their voice intelligibility. In order to preserve their voice individuality, we use a "combined-dictionary" that consists of a source speaker's vowels and target speaker's consonants.

We replace the target dictionary $\mathbf{A}^s$ in Fig. 1 with the "combined-dictionary". Input source features $\mathbf{X}^s$, which consist of an articulation-disordered spectrum and its segment features, are decomposed into a linear combination of bases from the source dictionary $\mathbf{A}^s$ by NMF. The weights of the bases are estimated as an activity $\mathbf{H}^s$. Therefore, the activity includes the weight information of input features for each basis. Then, the activity is multiplied by a combined-dictionary in order to obtain converted spectral features $\hat{\mathbf{X}}^t$, which are represented by a linear combination of bases from the source speaker's vowels and target speaker's consonants. Because the source and target are parallel phonemically, the bases used in the converted features are phonemically the same as that of the source features.

3.3 Problems

In the NMF-based approach described in Sec. 3.2, the parallel dictionary consists of the parallel training data themselves. Therefore, as the number of the bases in the dictionary increases, the input signal comes to be represented by a linear combination of a large number of bases rather than a small number of bases. When the number of bases that represent the input signal becomes large, the assumption of similarity between source and target activities may be weak due to the influence of the mismatch between the input signal and the selected bases. Moreover, in the case of a combined-dictionary, the input articulation-disordered spectrum may come to be represented by a combination of vowels and consonants. We assume that this problem degrades the performance of our exemplar-based VC. Hence, we use a phoneme-categorized sub-dictionary in place of the large dictionary in order to reduce the number of the bases that represent the input signal and avoid the mixture of vowels and consonants.

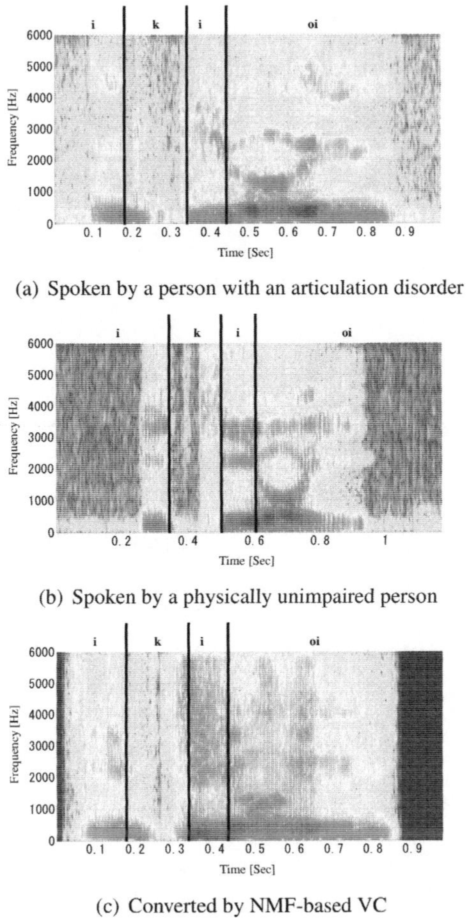

(a) Spoken by a person with an articulation disorder

(b) Spoken by a physically unimpaired person

(c) Converted by NMF-based VC

Figure 3: Examples of spectrogram //i k i oi

4 Non-negative Matrix Factorization Using a Phoneme-categorized Dictionary

4.1 Phoneme-categorized Dictionary

Fig. 4 shows how to construct the sub-dictionary. $\mathbf{A}^s$ and $\mathbf{A}^t$ imply the source and target dictionary which hold all the bases from training data. These dictionaries are divided into K dictionaries. In this paper, the dictionaries are divided into 10 categories according to the Japanese phoneme categories shown in Table 1.

In order to select the sub-dictionary, a "categorizing-dictionary", which consists of the representative vector from each sub-dictionary, is constructed. The representative vectors for each phoneme category consist of the mean vectors of the Gaussian Mixture Model (GMM).

$$p(\mathbf{x}_n^{(k)}) = \sum_{m=1}^{M_k} \alpha_m^{(k)} N(\mathbf{x}_n^{(k)}, \boldsymbol{\mu}_m^{(k)}, \boldsymbol{\Sigma}_m^{(k)}) \quad (4)$$

M_k, $\alpha_m^{(k)}$, $\boldsymbol{\mu}_m^{(k)}$ and $\boldsymbol{\Sigma}_m^{(k)}$ represent the number of the Gaussian mixture, the weights of mixture, mean and variance of the m-th mixture of the Gaussian, in the k-th sub-dictionary, respectively. Each parameter is estimated by using an EM algorithm.

The basis of the categorizing-dictionary, which corresponds to the k-th sub-dictionary $\boldsymbol{\Phi}_k^s$, is represented using the estimated phoneme GMM as follows:

$$\boldsymbol{\theta}_k = [\boldsymbol{\mu}_1^{(k)}, \ldots, \boldsymbol{\mu}_{M_k}^{(k)}] \quad (5)$$

$$\boldsymbol{\Phi}_k^s = [\mathbf{x}_1^{(k)}, \ldots, \mathbf{x}_{N_k}^{(k)}] \quad (6)$$

N_k represents the number of frames of the k-th sub-dictionary. The categorizing-dictionary $\boldsymbol{\Theta}$ is given as follows:

$$\boldsymbol{\Theta} = [\boldsymbol{\theta}_1, \ldots, \boldsymbol{\theta}_K] \quad (7)$$

4.2 Dictionary Selection and Voice Conversion

Fig. 5 shows the flow of the dictionary selection and VC. The input spectral features $\mathbf{X}^s$ are represented by a linear combination of bases from the categorizing-dictionary $\boldsymbol{\Theta}$. The weights of the

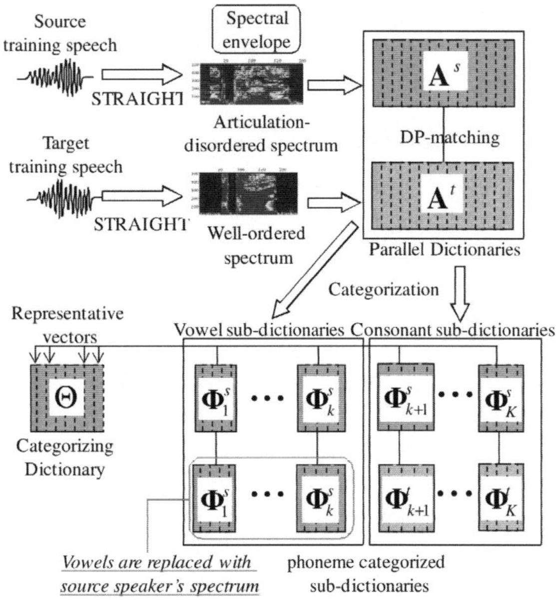

Figure 4: Making a sub-dictionary

bases are represented as activities $\mathbf{H}^s_{\mathbf{\Theta}}$.

$$\mathbf{X}^s \approx \mathbf{\Theta}\mathbf{H}^s_{\mathbf{\Theta}} \quad s.t. \quad \mathbf{H}^s_{\mathbf{\Theta}} \geq 0 \tag{8}$$

$$\mathbf{X}^s = [\mathbf{x}^s_1, \ldots, \mathbf{x}^s_L] \tag{9}$$

$$\mathbf{H}^s_{\mathbf{\Theta}} = [\mathbf{h}^s_{\mathbf{\Theta}1}, \ldots, \mathbf{h}^s_{\mathbf{\Theta}L}] \tag{10}$$

$$\mathbf{h}^s_{\mathbf{\Theta}l} = [\mathbf{h}^s_{\boldsymbol{\theta}_1 l}, \ldots, \mathbf{h}^s_{\boldsymbol{\theta}_K l}]^T \tag{11}$$

$$\mathbf{h}^s_{\boldsymbol{\theta}_k l} = [h^s_{\boldsymbol{\theta}_1 l}, \ldots, h^s_{\boldsymbol{\theta}_{M_k} l}]^T \tag{12}$$

Then, the l-th frame of input feature $\mathbf{x}^s_l$ is represented by a linear combination of bases from the sub-dictionary of the source speaker. The sub-dictionary $\mathbf{\Phi}^s_{\hat{k}}$, which corresponds to $\mathbf{x}_l$, is selected as follows:

$$\begin{aligned} \hat{k} &= \arg\max_k \mathbf{1}^{1\times M_k}\mathbf{h}^s_{\boldsymbol{\theta}_k l} \\ &= \arg\max_k \sum_{m=1}^{M_k} h^s_{\boldsymbol{\theta}_m l} \end{aligned} \tag{13}$$

$$\mathbf{x}_l = \mathbf{\Phi}^s_{\hat{k}}\mathbf{h}_{\hat{k},l} \tag{14}$$

The activity $\mathbf{h}_{l,\hat{k}}$ in Eq. (14) is estimated from the selected source speaker sub-dictionary.

If the selected sub-dictionary $\mathbf{\Phi}^s_{\hat{k}}$ is related to consonants, the l-th frame of the converted spectral feature $\hat{\mathbf{y}}_l$ is constructed by using the activity and the sub-dictionary of the target speaker $\mathbf{\Phi}^t_{\hat{k}}$.

$$\hat{\mathbf{y}}_l = \mathbf{\Phi}^t_{\hat{k}}\mathbf{h}_{\hat{k},l} \tag{15}$$

On the other hand, if the selected sub-dictionary $\mathbf{\Phi}^s_{\hat{k}}$ is related to vowels, the l-th frame of the converted spectral feature $\hat{\mathbf{y}}_l$ is constructed by using the activity and the sub-dictionary of the source speaker $\mathbf{\Phi}^s_{\hat{k}}$.

$$\hat{\mathbf{y}}_l = \mathbf{\Phi}^s_{\hat{k}}\mathbf{h}_{\hat{k},l} \tag{16}$$

Table 1: Japanese phoneme categories

	Category	phoneme
vowels	a	a
	e	e
	i	i
	o	o
	u	u
consonants	plosives	Q, b, d, dy, g, gy, k, ky, p, t
	fricatives	ch, f, h, hy, j, s, sh, ts, z
	nasals	m, my ny, N
	semivowels	w,y
	liquid	r, ry

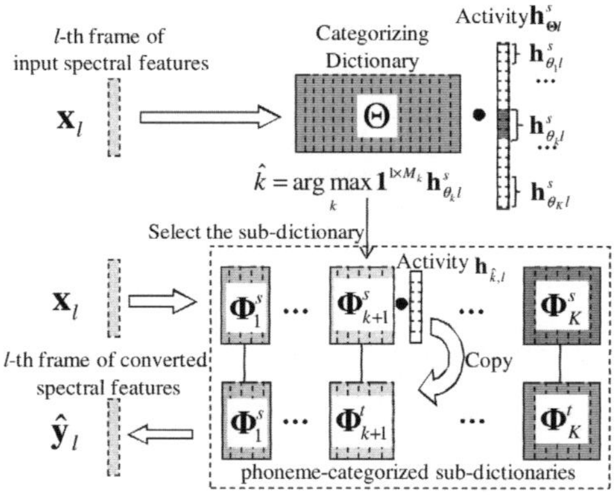

Figure 5: NMF-based voice conversion using categorized dictionary

5 Experimental Results

5.1 Experimental Conditions

The proposed VC technique was evaluated by comparing it with the conventional NMF-based method (Aihara et al., 2014) (referred to as the "sample-based method" in this paper) and the conventional GMM-based method (Stylianou et al., 1998) using clean speech data. We recorded 432 utterances (216 words, each repeated two times) included in the ATR Japanese speech database (Kurematsu et al., 1990). The speech signals were sampled at 12 kHz and windowed with a 25-msec Hamming window every 10 msec. A physically unimpaired Japanese male in the ATR Japanese speech database, was chosen as a target speaker.

In the proposed and sample-based methods, the number of dimensions of the spectral feature is 2,565. It consists of a 513-dimensional STRAIGHT spectrum (Kawahara et al., 1999) and its consecutive frames (the 2 frames coming before and the 2 frames coming after). The Gaussian mixture, which is used to construct a categorizing-dictionary, is 1/500 of the number of bases of each sub-dictionary. The number of iterations for estimating the activity in the proposed and sample-based methods was 300. In the conventional GMM-based method, MFCC+ΔMFCC+$\Delta\Delta$MFCC is used as a spectral feature. Its number of dimensions is 74. The number of Gaussian mixtures is set to 64, which is experimentally selected.

In this paper, F0 information is converted using a conventional linear regression based on the mean and standard deviation (Toda et al., 2007). The other information such as aperiodic components, is synthesized without any conversion.

We conducted a subjective evaluation of 3 topics. A total of 10 Japanese speakers took part in the test using headphones. For the "listening intelligibility" evaluation, we performed a MOS (Mean Opinion Score) test ("INTERNATIONAL TELECOMMUNICATION UNION", 2003). The opinion score was set to a 5-point scale (5: excellent, 4: good, 3: fair, 2: poor, 1: bad). Twenty-two words that are difficult for a person with an articulation disorder to utter were evaluated. The subjects were asked about the listening intelligibility in the articulation-disordered voice, the voice converted by our proposed method, and the GMM-based converted voice.

On the "similarity" evaluation, the XAB test was carried out. In the XAB test, each subject listened to the articulation-disordered voice. Then the subject listened to the voice converted by the two methods and selected which sample sounded most similar to the articulation-disordered voice. On the "naturalness" evaluation, a paired comparison test was carried out, where each subject listened to pairs of speech converted by the two methods and selected which sample sounded more natural.

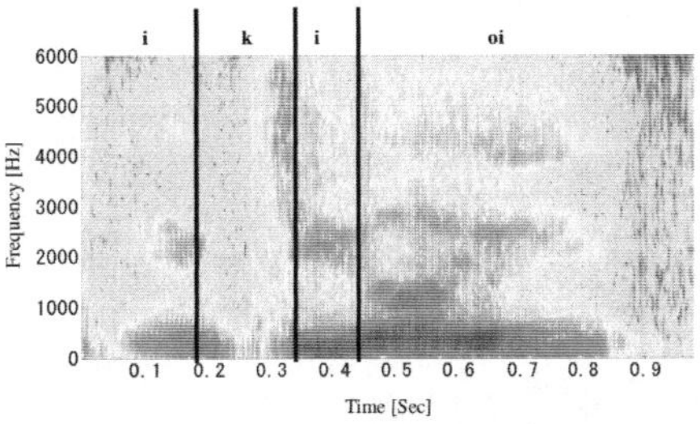

(a) Converted by proposed method

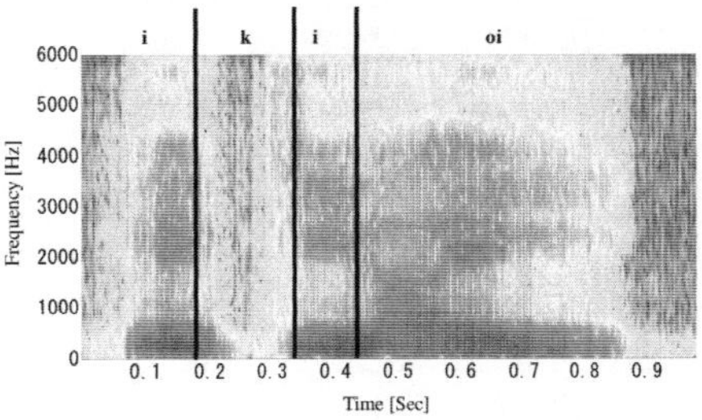

(b) Converted by GMM-based VC

Figure 6: Examples of converted spectrogram //i k i oi

5.2 Results and Discussion

Fig. 6(a) and 6(b) show examples of converted spectrograms using our proposed method and the conventional GMM-based method, respectively. In Fig. 6(a), there are fewer misconversions in the vowel part compared to Fig. 3(c). Moreover, by using GMM-based conversion, the area labeled "oi" becomes unclear compared to NMF-based conversion.

Fig. 7 shows the results of the MOS test for listening intelligibility. The error bars show a 95% confidence score; thus, our proposed VC method is shown to be able to improve the listening intelligibility and clarity of consonants. On the other hand, GMM-based conversion can improve the clarity of consonants, but it deteriorates the listening intelligibility. This is because GMM-based conversion has the effect of noise resulting from measurement error. Our proposed VC method also has the effect of noise, but it is less than that created by GMM-based conversion.

Fig. 8 shows the results of the XAB test on the similarity to the source speaker and naturalness of the converted voice. The error bars show a 95% confidence score. Our proposed VC method obtained a higher score than Sample-based and GMM-based conversion on similarity. Fig. 9

shows the preference score on the naturalness. The error bars show a 95% confidence score. Our proposed VC also method obtained a higher score than Sample-based and GMM-based conversion methods in regard to naturalness.

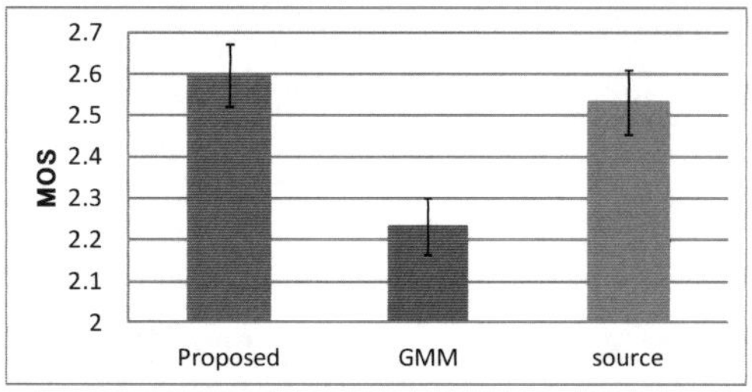

Figure 7: Results of MOS test on listening intelligibility

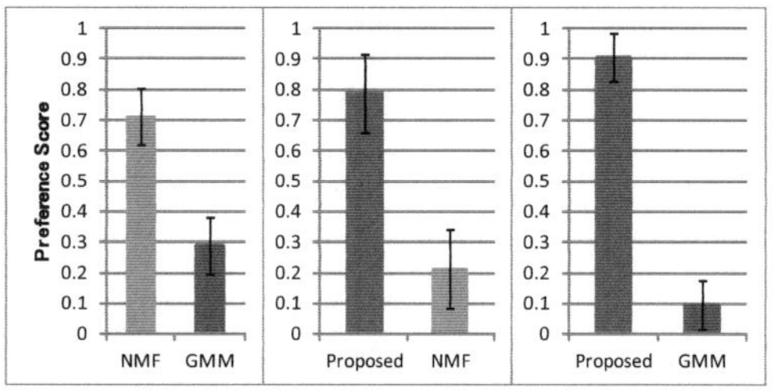

Figure 8: Preference scores for the individuality

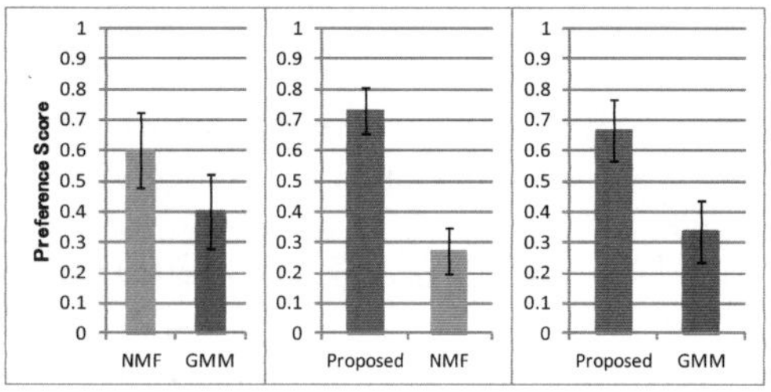

Figure 9: Preference scores for the naturalness

6 Conclusion

We proposed a spectral conversion method based on NMF for a voice with an articulation disorder. Our proposed method introduced a dictionary-selection method for conventional NMF-based VC. Experimental results demonstrated that our VC method can improve the listening intelligibility of words uttered by a person with an articulation disorder. Moreover, compared to conventional GMM-based VC and conventional NMF-based VC, our proposed VC method can preserve the individuality of the source speaker's voice and the naturalness of the voice. In this study, there was only one subject person, so in future experiments, we will increase the number of subjects and further examine the effectiveness of our method.

References

R. Aihara, R. Takashima, T. Takiguchi, and Y. Ariki. 2014. A preliminary demonstration of exemplar-based voice conversion for articulation disorders using an individuality-preserving dictionary. *EURASIP Journal on Audio, Speech, and Music Processing, 2014:5, doi:10.1186/1687-4722-2014-5.*

S. T. Canale and W. C. Campbell. 2002. Campbell's operative orthopaedics. Technical report, Mosby-Year Book.

J. F. Gemmeke, T. Viratnen, and A. Hurmalainen. 2011. Exemplar-based sparse representations for noise robust automatic speech recognition. *IEEE Trans. Audio, Speech and Language Processing, vol. 19, no. 7*, pages 2067–2080.

E. Helander, T. Virtanen, J. Nurminen, and M. Gabbouj. 2010. Voice conversion using partial least squares regression. *IEEE Trans. Audio, Speech, Lang. Process., vol. 18, Issue:5*, pages 912–921.

Mads Vilhelm Hollegaard, Kristin Skogstrand, Poul Thorsen, Bent Norgaard-Pedersen, David Michael Hougaard, and Jakob Grove. 2013. Joint analysis of SNPs and proteins identifies regulatory IL18 gene variations decreasing the chance of spastic cerebral palsy. *Human Mutation, Vol. 34*, pages 143–148.

INTERNATIONAL TELECOMMUNICATION UNION. 2003. Methods for objective and subjective assessment of quality. *ITU-T Recommendation P.800.*

A. Kain and M. W. Macon. 1998. Spectral voice conversion for text-to-speech synthesis. *in ICASSP, vol. 1*, pages 285–288.

H. Kawahara, I. Masuda-Katsuse, and A.de Cheveigne. 1999. Restructuring speech representations using a pitch-adaptive time-frequency smoothing and an instantaneous-frequencybased F0 extraction: possible role of a repetitive structure in sounds. *Speech Communication*, 27(3-4):187–207.

A. Kurematsu, K. Takeda, Y. Sagisaka, S. Katagiri, H. Kuwabara, and K. Shikano. 1990. ATR Japanese speech database as a tool of speech recognition and synthesis. *Speech Communication*, 9:357–363.

C. H. Lee and C. H. Wu. 2006. Map-based adaptation for speech conversion using adaptation data selection and non-parallel training. *in Interspeech*, pages 2254–2257.

H. Matsumasa, T. Takiguchi, Y. Ariki, I. Li, and T. Nakabayachi. 2009. Integration of metamodel and acoustic model for dysarthric speech recognition. *Journal of Multimedia, Volume 4, Issue 4*, pages 254–261.

K. Nakamura, T. Toda, H. Saruwatari, and K. Shikano. 2006. Speaking aid system for total laryngectomees using voice conversion of body transmitted artificial speech. *in Interspeech*, pages 148–151.

K. Nakamura, T. Toda, H. Saruwatari, and K. Shikano. 2012. Speaking-aid systems using GMM-based voice conversion for electrolaryngeal speech. *Speech Communication*, 54(1):134–146.

F. Rudzicz. 2011. Acoustic transformations to improve the intelligibility of dysarthric speech. *in proc. the Second Workshop on Speech and Language Processing for Assistive Technologies*.

F. Rudzicz. 2014. Adjusting dysarthric speech signals to be more intelligible. *in Computer Speech and Language, 27(6), September*, pages 1163–1177.

Y. Stylianou, O. Cappe, and E. Moilines. 1998. Continuous probabilistic transform for voice conversion. *IEEE Trans. Speech and Audio Processing*, 6(2):131–142.

R. Takashima, T. Takiguchi, and Y. Ariki. 2012. Exemplar-based voice conversion in noisy environment. *in SLT*, pages 313–317.

T. Toda, Y. Ohtani, and K. Shikano. 2006. Eigenvoice conversion based on Gaussian mixture model. *in Interspeech*, pages 2446–2449.

T. Toda, A. Black, and K. Tokuda. 2007. Voice conversion based on maximum likelihood estimation of spectral parameter trajectory. *IEEE Trans. Audio, Speech, Lang. Process.*, 15(8):2222–2235.

H. Valbret, E. Moulines, and J. P. Tubach. 1992. Voice transformation using PSOLA technique. *Speech Communication, vol. 11, no. 2-3, pp. 175-187*.

C. Veaux and X. Robet. 2011. Intonation conversion from neutral to expressive speech. *in Interspeech*, pages 2765–2768.

C. Veaux, J. Yamagishi, and S. King. 2012. Using HMM-based speech synthesis to reconstruct the voice of individuals with degenerative speech disorders. *in Interspeech*, pages 1–4.

J. Yamagishi, Christophe Veaux, Simon King, and Steve Renals. 2013. Speech synthesis technologies for individuals with vocal disabilities: Voice banking and reconstruction. *Acoustical Science and Technology, Vol. 33 (2012) No. 1*, pages 1–5.

Preliminary Test of a Real-Time, Interactive Silent Speech Interface Based on Electromagnetic Articulograph

Jun Wang
Dept. of Bioengineering
Callier Center for Communication Disorders
University of Texas at Dallas
wangjun@utdallas.edu

Ashok Samal
Dept. of Computer Science & Engineering
University of Nebraska-Lincoln
samal@cse.unl.edu

Jordan R. Green
Dept. of Communication Sciences & Disorders
MGH Institute of Health Professions
jgreen2@mghihp.edu

Abstract

A silent speech interface (SSI) maps articulatory movement data to speech output. Although still in experimental stages, silent speech interfaces hold significant potential for facilitating oral communication in persons after laryngectomy or with other severe voice impairments. Despite the recent efforts on silent speech recognition algorithm development using offline data analysis, online test of SSIs have rarely been conducted. In this paper, we present a preliminary, online test of a real-time, interactive SSI based on electromagnetic motion tracking. The SSI played back synthesized speech sounds in response to the user's tongue and lip movements. Three English talkers participated in this test, where they mouthed (silently articulated) phrases using the device to complete a phrase-reading task. Among the three participants, 96.67% to 100% of the mouthed phrases were correctly recognized and corresponding synthesized sounds were played after a short delay. Furthermore, one participant demonstrated the feasibility of using the SSI for a short conversation. The experimental results demonstrated the feasibility and potential of silent speech interfaces based on electromagnetic articulograph for future clinical applications.

1 Introduction

Daily communication is often a struggle for persons who have undergone a laryngectomy, a surgical removal of the larynx due to the treatment of cancer (Bailey et al., 2006). In 2013, about 12,260 new cases of laryngeal cancer were estimated in the United States (American Cancer Society, 2013). Currently, there are only limited treatment options for these individuals including (1) esophageal speech, which involves oscillation of the esophagus and is difficult to learn; (2) tracheo-esophageal speech, in which a voice prosthesis is placed in a tracheo-esophageal puncture; and (3) electrolarynx, an external device held on the neck during articulation, which produces a robotic voice quality (Liu and Ng, 2007). Perhaps the greatest disadvantage of these approaches is that they produce abnormal sounding speech with a fundamental frequency that is low and limited in range. The abnormal voice quality output severely affects the social life of people after laryngectomy (Liu and Ng, 2007). In addition, the tracheo-esophageal option requires an additional surgery, which is not suitable for every patient (Bailey et al., 2006). Although research is being conducted on improving the voice quality of esophageal or electrolarynx speech (Doi et al., 2010; Toda et al., 2012), new assistive technologies based on non-audio information (e.g., visual or articulatory information) may be a good alternative approach for providing natural sounding speech output for persons after laryngectomy.

Visual speech recognition (or automatic lip reading) typically uses an optical camera to obtain lip and/or facial features during speech (including lip contour, color, opening, movement, etc.) and then classify these features to speech units (Meier et al., 2000; Oviatt, 2003). However, due to the lack of information from tongue, the primary articulator, visual speech recognition (i.e., using visual information only, without tongue and audio information) may obtain a low accuracy (e.g., 30% - 40% for phoneme classification, Livescu et al., 2007). Furthermore, Wang and colleagues (2013b) have showed any single tongue sensor (from tongue tip to tongue body

Proceedings of the 5th Workshop on Speech and Language Processing for Assistive Technologies (SLPAT), pages 38–45,
Baltimore, Maryland USA, August 26 2014.

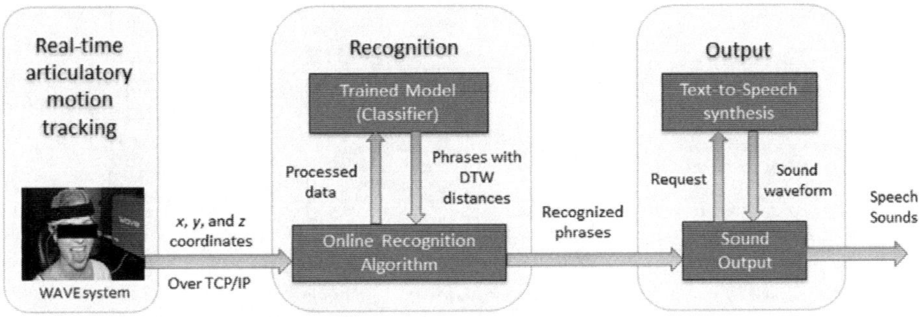

Figure 1. Design of the real-time silent speech interface.

back on the midsagittal line) encodes significantly more information in distinguishing phonemes than do lips. However, visual speech recognition is well suited for applications with small-vocabulary (e.g., a lip-reading based command-and-control system for home appliance) or using visual information as an additional source for acoustic speech recognition, referred to as audio-visual speech recognition (Potamianos et al., 2003), because such a system based on portable camera is convenient in practical use. In contrast, SSIs, with tongue information, have potential to obtain a high level of silent speech recognition accuracy (without audio information). Currently, two major obstacles for SSI development are lack of (a) fast and accurate recognition algorithms and (b) portable tongue motion tracking devices for daily use.

SSIs convert articulatory information into text that drives a text-to-speech synthesizer. Although still in developmental stages (e.g., speaker-dependent recognition, small-vocabulary), SSIs even have potential to provide speech output based on prerecorded samples of the patient's own voice (Denby et al., 2010; Green et al., 2011; Wang et al., 2009). Potential articulatory data acquisition methods for SSIs include ultrasound (Denby et al., 2011; Hueber et al., 2010), surface electromyography electrodes (Heaton et al., 2011; Jorgensen and Dusan, 2010), and electromagnetic articulograph (EMA) (Fagan et al., 2008; Wang et al., 2009, 2012a).

Despite the recent effort on silent speech interface research, online test of SSIs has rarely been studied. So far, most of the published work on SSIs has focused on development of silent speech recognition algorithm through offline analysis (i.e., using prerecorded data) (Fagan et al., 2008; Heaton et al., 2011; Hofe et al., 2013; Hueber et al., 2010; Jorgenson et al., 2010; Wang et al., 2009a, 2012a, 2012b, 2013c). Ultrasound-based SSIs have been tested online with multiple subjects and encouraging results were obtained in a phrase reading task where the subjects were asked to silently articulate sixty phrases (Denby et al., 2011). SSI based on electromagnetic sensing has been only tested using offline analysis (using pre-recorded data) collected from single subjects (Fagan et al., 2008; Hofe et al., 2013), although some work simulated online testing using prerecorded data (Wang et al., 2012a, 2012b, 2013c). Online tests of SSIs using electromagnetic articulograph with multiple subjects are needed to show the feasibility and potential of the SSIs for future clinical applications.

In this paper, we report a preliminary, online test of a newly-developed, real-time, and interactive SSI based on a commercial EMA. EMA tracks articulatory motion by placing small sensors on the surface of tongue and other articulators (e.g., lips and jaw). EMA is well suited for the early state of SSI development because it (1) is non-invasive, (2) has a high spatial resolution in motion tracking, (3) has a high sampling rate, and (4) is affordable. In this experiment, participants used the real-time SSI to complete an online phrase-reading task and one of them had a short conversation with another person. The results demonstrated the feasibility and potential of SSIs based on electromagnetic sensing for future clinical applications.

2 Design

2.1 Major design

Figure 1 illustrates the three-component design of the SSI: (a) real-time articulatory motion tracking using a commercial EMA, (b) online silent speech recognition (converting articulation information to text), and (c) text-to-speech synthesis for speech output.

The EMA system (Wave Speech Research

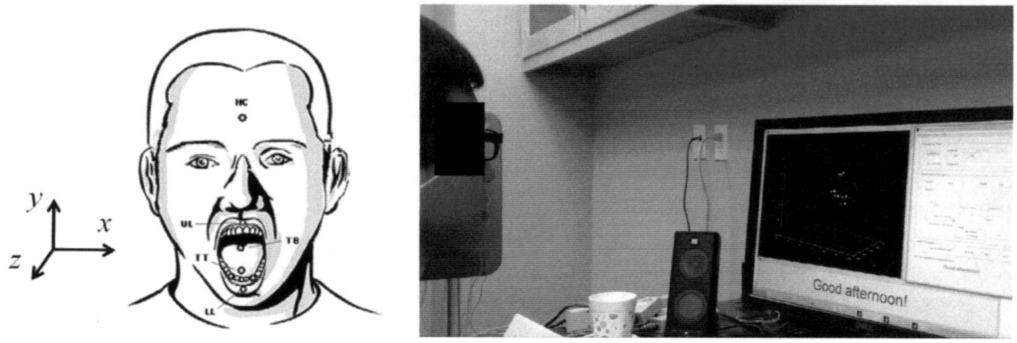

Figure 2. Demo of a participant using the silent speech interface. The left picture illustrates the coordinate system and sensor locations (sensor labels are described in text); in the right picture, a participant is using the silent speech interface to finish the online test.

system, Northern Digital Inc., Waterloo, Canada) was used to track the tongue and lip movement in real-time. The sampling rate of the Wave system was 100 Hz, which is adequate for this application (Wang et al., 2012a, 2012b, 2013c). The spatial accuracy of motion tracking using Wave is 0.5 mm (Berry, 2011).

The online recognition component recognized functional phrases from articulatory movements in real-time. The recognition component is modular such that alternative classifiers can easily replace and be integrated into the SSI. In this preliminary test, recognition was speaker-dependent, where training and testing data were from the same speakers.

The third component played back either pre-recorded or synthesized sounds using a text-to-speech synthesizer (Huang et al., 1997).

2.2 Other designs

A *graphical user interface* (GUI) is integrated into the silent speech interface for ease of operation. Using the GUI, users can instantly re-train the recognition engine (classifier) when new training samples are available. Users can also switch output voice (e.g., male or female).

Data transfer through TCP/IP. Data transfer from the Wave system to the recognition unit (software) is accomplished through TCP/IP, the standard data transfer protocols on Internet. Because data bandwidth requirement is low (multiple sensors, multiple spatial coordinates for each sensor, at 100 Hz sampling rate), any 3G or faster network connection will be sufficient for future use with wireless data transfer.

Extensible (closed) vocabulary. In the early stage of this development, closed-vocabulary silent speech recognition was used; however, the vocabulary is extensible. Users can add new phrases into the system through the GUI. Adding a new phrase in the vocabulary is done in two steps. The user (the patient) first enters the phrase using a keyboard (keyboard input can also be done by an assistant or speech pathologist), and then produces a few training samples for the phrase (a training sample is articulatory data labeled with a phrase). The system automatically re-trains the recognition model integrating the newly-added training samples. Users can delete invalid training samples using the GUI as well.

2.3 Real-time data processing

The tongue and lip movement positional data obtained from the Wave system were processed in real-time prior to being used for recognition. This included the calculation of head-independent positions of the tongue and lip sensors and low pass filtering for removing noise.

The movements of the 6 DOF head sensor were used to calculate the head-independent movements of other sensors. The Wave system represents object orientation or rotation (denoted by *yaw*, *pitch*, and *roll* in Euler angles) in quaternions, a four-dimensional vector. Quaternion has its advantages over Euler angles. For example, quaternion avoids the issue of gimbal lock (one degree of freedom may be lost in a series of rotation), and it is simpler to achieve smooth interpolation using quaternion than using Euler angles (Dam et al., 1998). Thus, quaternion has been widely used in computer graphics, computer vision, robotics, virtual reality, and flight dynamics (Kuipers, 1999). Given the unit quaternion

$$q = (a, b, c, d) \qquad (1)$$

where $a^2 + b^2 + c^2 + d^2 = 1$, a 3×3 rotation matrix R can be derived using Equation (2):

$$R = \begin{bmatrix} a^2+b^2-c^2-d^2 & 2bc-2ad & 2bd+2ac \\ 2bc+2ad & a^2-b^2+c^2-d^2 & 2cd-2ab \\ 2bd-2ac & 2cd+2ab & a^2-b^2-c^2+d^2 \end{bmatrix} \quad (2)$$

For details of how the quaternion is used in Wave system, please refer to the Wave Real-Time API manual and sample application (Northern Digital Inc., Waterloo, Canada).

3 A Preliminary Online Test

3.1 Participants & Stimuli

Three American English talkers participated in this experiment (two males and one female with average age 25 and SD 3.5 years). No history of speech, language, hearing, or any cognitive problems were reported.

Sixty phrases that are frequently used in daily life by healthy people and AAC (augmentative and alternative communication) users were used in this experiment. Those phrases were selected from the lists in Wang et al., 2012a and Beukelman and Gutmann, 1999.

3.2 Procedure

Setup

The Wave system tracks the motion of sensors attached on the articulators by establishing an electromagnetic field by a textbook-sized generator. Participants were seated with their head within the calibrated magnetic field (Figure 2, the right picture), facing a computer monitor that displays the GUI of the SSI. The sensors were attached to the surface of each articulator using dental glue (PeriAcryl Oral Tissue Adhesive). Prior to the experiment, each subject participated in a three-minute training session (on how to use the SSI), which also helped them adapt to the oral sensors. Previous studies have shown those sensors do not significantly affect their speech output after a short practice (Katz et al., 2006; Weismer and Bunton, 1999).

Figure 2 (left) shows the positions of the five sensors attached to a participant's forehead, tongue, and lips (Green et al., 2003; 2013; Wang et al., 2013a). One 6 DOF (spatial and rotational) head sensor was attached to a nose bridge on a pair of glasses (rather than on forehead skin directly), to avoid the skin artifact (Green et al., 2007). Two 5 DOF sensors - TT (Tongue Tip) and TB (Tongue Body Back) - were attached on the midsagittal of the tongue. TT was located approximately 10 mm from the tongue apex (Wang et al., 2011, 2013a). TB was placed as far back as possible, depending on the participant's tongue length (Wang et al., 2013b). Lip movements were captured by attaching two 5 DOF sensors to the vermilion borders of the upper (UL) and lower (LL) lips at midline. The four sensors (i.e., TT, TB, UL, and LL) placements were selected based on literature showing that they are able to achieve as high recognition accuracy as that obtained using more tongue sensors for this application (Wang et al., 2013b).

As mentioned previously, real-time preprocessing of the positional time series was conducted, including subtraction of head movements from tongue and lip data and noise reduction using a 20 Hz low pass filter (Green et al., 2003; Wang et al., 2013a). Although the tongue and lip sensors are 5D, only the 3D spatial data (i.e., x, y, and z) were used in this experiment.

Training

The training step was conducted to obtain a few samples for each phrase. The participants were asked to silently articulate all sixty phrases twice at their comfortable speaking rate, while the tongue and lip motion was recorded. Thus, each phrase has at least two samples for training. Dynamic Time Warping (DTW) was used as the classifier in this preliminary test, because of its rapid execution (Denby et al., 2011), although Gaussian mixture models may perform well too when the number of training samples is small (Broekx et al., 2013). DTW is typically used to compare two single-dimensional time-series,

Training_Algorithm

Let $T_1 \ldots T_n$ be the sets of training samples for n phrases, where $T_i = \{T_{i,1}, \ldots T_{i,j}, \ldots T_{i,mi}\}$ are m_i samples for phrase i.

for $i = 1$ **to** n // n is the number of phrases
    $L_i = \text{sum}(\text{length}(T_{i,j})) / m_i$, $j = 1$ to m_i;
    $T = T_{i,1}$; // first sample of phrase i
    for $j = 2$ **to** m_i
        $(T', T'_{i,j}) = \text{MDTW}(T, T_{i,j})$;
        $T = (T' + T'_{i,j}) / 2$; //amplitude mean
        $T = \text{time\_normalize}(T, L_i)$;
    end
    $R_i = T$; // representative sample for phrase i
end
Output(R);

Figure 3. Training algorithm using DTW. The function call MDTW() returns the average DTW distances between the corresponding sensors and dimensions of two data samples.

thus we calculated the average DTW distance across the corresponding sensors and dimensions of two data samples. DTW was adapted as follows for training.

The training algorithm generated a *representative* sample based on all available training samples for each phrase. Pseudo-code of the training algorithm is provided in Figure 3, for the convenience of description. For each phrase i, first, MDTW was applied to the first two training samples, $T_{i,1}$ and $T_{i,2}$. Sample T is the amplitude-mean of the warped samples $T'_{i,1}$ and $T'_{i,2}$ (time-series) (Line 5). Next, T was time-normalized (stretched) to the average length of all training samples for this phrase (L_i), which was to reduce the effects of duration change caused by DTW warping (Line 6). The procedure continued until the last training sample $T_{i,mi}$ (m_i is the number of training samples for phrase i). The final T was the representative sample for phrase i.

The training procedure can be initiated by pressing a button on the GUI anytime during the use of the SSI.

Testing

During testing, each participant silently articulated the same list of phrases while the SSI recognized each phrase and played corresponding synthesized sounds. DTW was used to compare the test sample with the representative training sample for each phrase (R_i, Figure 3). The phrase that had the shortest DTW distance to the test sample was recognized. The testing was triggered by pressing a button on the GUI. If the phrase was incorrectly predicted, the participant was allowed to add *at most* two additional training samples for that phrase.

Figure 2 (right) demonstrates a participant is using the SSI during the test. After the participant silently articulated "*Good afternoon*", the SSI displayed the phrase on the screen, and played the corresponding synthesized sound simultaneously.

Finally, one participant used the SSI for a bidirectional conversation with an investigator. Since this prototype SSI has a closed-vocabulary recognition component, the participant had to choose the phrases that have been trained. This task was intended to provide a demo of how the SSI is used for daily communication. The script of the conversation is as below:

Investigator: *Hi DJ, How are you?*
Subject: *I'm fine. How are you doing?*
Investigator: *I'm good. Thanks.*
Subject: *I use a silent speech interface to talk.*
Investigator: *That's cool.*
Subject: *Do you understand me?*
Investigator: *Oh, yes.*
Subject: *That's good.*

Subject	Accuracy (%)	Latency (s)	# of Training Samples
S01	100	3.086	2.0
S02	96.67	1.403	2.4
S03	96.67	1.524	3.1

Table 1. Phrase classification accuracy and latency for all three participants.

4 Results and Discussion

Table 1 lists the performance using the SSI for all three participants in the online, phrase-reading task. The three subjects obtained a phrase recognition accuracy from 96.67% to 100.00%, with a latency from 1.403 second to 3.086 seconds, respectively. The high accuracy and relatively short delay demonstrated the feasibility and potential of SSIs based on electromagnetic articulograph.

The order of the participants in the experiment was S01, S02, and then S03. After the experiment of S01, where all three dimensional data (x, y, and z) were used, we decided to use only y and z for S02 and S03 to reduce the latency. As listed in Table 1, the latencies of S02 and S03 did significantly reduce, because less data was used for online recognition.

Surprisingly, phrase recognition without using x dimension (left-right) data led to a decrease of accuracy and more training samples were required; prior research suggests that tongue movement in this dimension is not significant during speech in healthy talkers (Westbury, 1994). This observation is supported by participant S01, who had the highest accuracy and needed fewer training samples for each phrase (column 3 in Table 1). S02 and S03 used data of only y and z dimensions. Of course, data from more subjects are needed to confirm the potential significance of the x dimension movement of the tongue to silent speech recognition accuracy.

Data transfer between the Wave machine and the SSI recognition component was done through TCP/IP protocols and in real-time. In the future, this design feature will allow the recognition component to run on a smart phone or any wearable devices with an Internet connection (Cellular or Wi-Fi). In this preliminary test, the individual delays caused by TCP/IP data transfer, online data preprocessing, and classification were not measured and thus unknown. The delay information may be useful for our future development that the recognition component is deployed on a smart-phone. A further study is needed to obtain and analyze the delay information.

The bidirectional dialogue by one of the participants demonstrated how the SSI can be used in daily conversation. To our best knowledge, this is the first conversational demo using a SSI. An informal survey to a few colleagues provided positive feedback. The conversation was smooth, although it is noticeably slower than a conversation between two healthy talkers. Importantly, the voice output quality (determined by the text-to-speech synthesizer) was natural, which strongly supports the major motivation of SSI research: to produce speech with natural voice quality that current treatments cannot provide. A video demo is available online (Wang, 2014).

The participants in this experiment were young and healthy. It is, however, unknown if the recognition accuracy may decrease or not for users after laryngectomy, although a single patient study showed the accuracy may decrease 15-20% compared to healthy talkers using an ultrasound-based SSI (Denby et al., 2011). Theoretically, the tongue motion patterns in (silent) speech after the surgery should be no difference with that of healthy talkers. In practice, however, some patients after the surgery may be under treatment for swallowing using radioactive devices, which may affect their tongue motion patterns in articulation. Thus, the performance of SSIs may vary and depend on the condition of the patients after laryngectomy. A test of the SSI using multiple participants after laryngectomy is needed to understand the performance of SSIs for those patients under different conditions.

Although a demonstration of daily conversation using the SSI is provided, SSI based on the non-portable Wave system is currently not ready for practical use. Fortunately, more affordable and portable electromagnetic devices are being developed as are small handheld or wearable devices (Fagan et al., 2008). Researchers are also testing the efficacy of permanently implantable and wireless sensors (Chen et al., 2012; Park et al., 2012). In the future, those more portable, and wireless articulatory motion tracking devices, when they are ready, will be used to develop a portable SSI for practice use.

In this experiment, a simple DTW algorithm was used to compare the training and testing phrases, which is known to be slower than most machine learning classifiers. Thus, in the future, the latency can be significantly reduced by using faster classifiers such as support vector machines (Wang et al., 2013c) or hidden Markov models (Heracleous and Hagita, 2011; King et al., 2007; Rudzicz et al., 2012; Uraga and Hain, 2006).

Furthermore, in this proof-of-concept design, the vocabulary was limited to a small set of phrases, because our design required the whole experiment (including training and testing) to be done in about one hour. Additional work is needed to test the feasibility of open-vocabulary recognition, which will be much more usable for people after laryngectomy or with other severe voice impairments.

5 Conclusion and Future Work

A preliminary, online test of a SSI based on electromagnetic articulograph was conducted. The results were encouraging revealing high phrase recognition accuracy and short playback latencies among three participants in a phrase-reading task. In addition, a proof-of-concept demo of bidirectional conversation using the SSI was provided, which shows how the SSI can be used for daily communication.

Future work includes: (1) testing the SSI with patients after laryngectomy or with severe voice impairment, (2) integrating a phoneme- or word-level recognition (open-vocabulary) using faster machine learning classifiers (e.g., support vector machines or hidden Markov models), and (3) exploring speaker-independent silent speech recognition algorithms by normalizing the articulatory movement across speakers (e.g., due to the anatomical difference of their tongues).

Acknowledgements

This work was in part supported by the Callier Excellence in Education Fund, University of Texas at Dallas, and grants awarded by the National Institutes of Health (R01 DC009890 and R01 DC013547). We would like to thank Dr. Thomas F. Campbell, Dr. William F. Katz, Dr. Gregory S. Lee, Dr. Jennell C. Vick, Lindsey Macy, Marcus Jones, Kristin J. Teplansky, Vedad "Kelly" Fazel, Loren Montgomery, and Kameron Johnson for their support or assistance. We also thank the anonymous reviewers for their comments and suggestions for improving the quality of this paper.

References

American Cancer Society. 2013. *Cancer Facts and Figures 2013*. American Cancer Society, Atlanta, GA. Retrieved on February 18, 2014.

Bailey, B. J., Johnson, J. T., and Newlands, S. D. 2006. *Head and Neck Surgery – Otolaryngology*, Lippincot, Williams & Wilkins, Philadelphia, PA, USA, 4th Ed., 1779-1780.

Berry, J. 2011. Accuracy of the NDI wave speech research system, *Journal of Speech, Language, and Hearing Research*, 54:1295-1301.

Beukelman, D. R., and Gutmann, M. 1999. Generic Message List for AAC users with ALS. http://aac.unl.edu/ALS_Message_List1.htm

Broekx, L., Dreesen, K., Gemmeke, J. F., and Van Hamme, H. 2013. Comparing and combining classifiers for self-taught vocal interfaces, *ACL/ISCA Workshop on Speech and Language Processing for Assistive Technologies*, 21-28, 2013.

Chen, W.-H., Loke, W.-F., Thompson, G., and Jung, B. 2012. A 0.5V, 440uW frequency synthesizer for implantable medical devices, *IEEE Journal of Solid-State Circuits*, 47:1896-1907.

Dam, E. B., Koch, M., and Lillholm, M. 1998. *Quaternions, interpolation and animation*. Technical Report DIKU-TR-98/5, University of Copenhagen.

Denby, B., Cai, J., Roussel, P., Dreyfus, G., Crevier-Buchman, L., Pillot-Loiseau, C., Hueber, and T., Chollet, G. 2011. Tests of an interactive, phrasebook-style post-laryngectomy voice-replacement system, *the 17th International Congress on Phonetic Sciences*, Hong Kong, China, 572-575.

Denby, B., Schultz, T., Honda, K., Hueber, T., Gilbert, J. M., and Brumberg, J. S. 2010. Silent speech interface, *Speech Communication*, 52:270-287.

Doi, H., Nakamura, K., Toda, T., Saruwatari, H., Shikano, K. 2010. Esophageal speech enhancement based on statistical voice conversion with Gaussian mixture models, *IEICE Transactions on Information and Systems*, E93-D, 9:2472-2482.

Fagan, M. J., Ell, S. R., Gilbert, J. M., Sarrazin, E., and Chapman, P. M. 2008. Development of a (silent) speech recognition system for patients following laryngectomy, *Medical Engineering & Physics*, 30(4):419-425.

Green, P. D., Khan, Z., Creer, S. M. and Cunningham, S. P. 2011. Reconstructing the voice of an individual following Laryngectomy, *Augmentative and Alternative Communication*, 27(1):61-66.

Green, J. R., Wang, J., and Wilson, D. L. 2013. SMASH: A tool for articulatory data processing and analysis, *Proc. Interspeech*, 1331-35.

Green, J. R. and Wang, Y. 2003. Tongue-surface movement patterns during speech and swallowing, *Journal of the Acoustical Society of America*, 113:2820-2833.

Hofe, R., Ell, S. R., Fagan, M. J., Gilbert, J. M., Green, P. D., Moore, R. K., and Rybchenko, S. I. 2013. Small-vocabulary speech recognition using a silent speech interface based on magnetic sensing, *Speech Communication*, 55(1):22-32.

Hofe, R., Ell, S. R., Fagan, M. J., Gilbert, J. M., Green, P. D., Moore, R. K., and Rybchenko, S. I. 2011. Speech Synthesis Parameter Generation for the Assistive Silent Speech Interface MVOCA, *Proc. Interspeech*, 3009-3012.

Huang, X. D., Acero, A., Hon, H.-W., Ju, Y.-C., Liu, J., Meredith, S., and Plumpe, M. 1997. Recent Improvements on Microsoft's Trainable Text-to-Speech System: Whistler, *Proc. IEEE Intl. Conf. on Acoustics, Speech, and Signal Processing*, 959-962.

Hueber, T., Benaroya, E.-L., Chollet, G., Denby, B., Dreyfus, G., Stone, M. 2010. Development of a silent speech interface driven by ultrasound and optical images of the tongue and lips, *Speech Communication*, 52:288–300.

Heaton, J. T., Robertson, M., and Griffin, C. 2011. Development of a wireless electromyographically controlled electrolarynx voice prosthesis, *Proc. of the 33rd Annual Intl. Conf. of the IEEE Engineering in Medicine & Biology Society*, Boston, MA, 5352-5355.

Heracleous, P., and Hagita, N. 2011. Automatic recognition of speech without any audio information, *Proc. IEEE Intl. Conf. on Acoustics, Speech, and Signal Processing*, 2392-2395.

Jorgensen, C. and Dusan, S. 2010. Speech interfaces based upon surface electromyography, *Speech Communication*, 52:354–366, 2010.

Katz, W., Bharadwaj, S., Rush, M., and Stettler, M. 2006. Influences of EMA receiver coils on speech production by normal and aphasic/apraxic talkers, *Journal of Speech, Language, and Hearing Research*, 49:645-659.

Kent, R. D., Adams, S. G., and Tuner, G. S. 1996. Models of speech production, in *Principles of Experimental Phonetics*, Ed., Lass, N. J., Mosby: St Louis, MO.

King, S., Frankel, J. Livescu, K., McDermott, E., Richmond, K., Wester, M. 2007. Speech production knowledge in automatic speech recognition, *Journal of the Acoustical Society of America*, 121(2):723-742.

Kuipers, J. B. 1999. *Quaternions and rotation Sequences: a Primer with Applications to Orbits, Aerospace, and Virtual Reality*, Princeton University Press, Princeton, NJ.

Liu, H., and Ng, M. L. 2007. Electrolarynx in voice rehabilitation, *Auris Nasus Larynx*, 34(3): 327-332.

Livescu, K., Çetin, O., Hasegawa-Johnson, Mark, King, S., Bartels, C., Borges, N., Kantor, A., et al. (2007). Articulatory feature-based methods for acoustic and audio-visual speech recognition: Summary from the 2006 JHU Summer Workshop. *Proc. IEEE Intl. Conf. on Acoustics, Speech, and Signal Processing*, 621-624.

Meier, U., Stiefelhagen, R., Yang, J., and Waibel, A. (2000). Towards Unrestricted Lip Reading. *International Journal of Pattern Recognition and Artificial Intelligence*, 14(5): 571-585.

Oviatt, S. L. 2003. Multimodal interfaces, in *Human–Computer Interaction Handbook: Fundamentals, Evolving Technologies and Emerging Applications*, Eds. Julie A. Jacko and Andrew Sears (Mahwah, NJ:Erlbaum): 286–304.

Park, H., Kiani, M., Lee, H. M., Kim, J., Block, J., Gosselin, B., and Ghovanloo, M. 2012. A wireless magnetoresistive sensing system for an intraoral tongue-computer interface, *IEEE Transactions on Biomedical Circuits and Systems*, 6(6):571-585.

Potamianos, G., Neti, C., Cravier, G., Garg, A. and Senior, A. W. 2003. Recent advances in the automatic recognition of audio-visual speech, *Proc. of IEEE*, 91(9):1306-1326.

Rudzicz, F., Hirst, G., Van Lieshout, P. 2012. Vocal tract representation in the recognition of cerebral palsied speech, *Journal of Speech, Language, and Hearing Research*, 55(4): 1190-1207.

Toda, T., Nakagiri, M., Shikano, K. 2012. Statistical voice conversion techniques for body-conducted unvoiced speech enhancement, *IEEE Transactions on Audio, Speech and Language Processing*, 20(9): 2505-2517.

Uraga, E. and Hain, T. 2006. Automatic speech recognition experiments with articulatory data, *Proc. Inerspeech*, 353-356.

Wang, J., Samal, A., Green, J. R., and Carrell, T. D. 2009. Vowel recognition from articulatory position time-series data, *Proc. IEEE Intl. Conf. on Signal Processing and Communication Systems*, Omaha, NE, 1-6.

Wang, J., Green, J. R., Samal, A., and Marx, D. B. 2011. Quantifying articulatory distinctiveness of vowels, *Proc. Interspeech*, Florence, Italy, 277-280.

Wang, J., Samal, A., Green, J. R., and Rudzicz, F. 2012a. Sentence recognition from articulatory movements for silent speech interfaces, *Proc. IEEE Intl. Conf. on Acoustics, Speech, and Signal Processing*, 4985-4988.

Wang, J., Samal, A., Green, J. R., and Rudzicz, F. 2012b. Whole-word recognition from articulatory movements for silent speech interfaces, *Proc. Interspeech*, 1327-30.

Wang, J., Green, J. R., Samal, A. and Yunusova, Y. 2013a. Articulatory distinctiveness of vowels and consonants: A data-driven approach, *Journal of Speech, Language, and Hearing Research*, 56, 1539-1551.

Wang, J., Green, J. R., and Samal, A. 2013b. Individual articulator's contribution to phoneme production, *Proc. IEEE Intl. Conf. on Acoustics, Speech, and Signal Processing*, Vancouver, Canada, 7795-89.

Wang, J., Balasubramanian, A., Mojica de La Vega, L., Green, J. R., Samal, A., and Prabhakaran, B. 2013c. Word recognition from continuous articulatory movement time-series data using symbolic representations, *ACL/ISCA Workshop on Speech and Language Processing for Assistive Technologies*, Grenoble, France, 119-127.

Wang J. 2014. DJ and his friend: A demo of conversation using a real-time silent speech interface based on electromagnetic articulograph. [Video]. Available: http://www.utdallas.edu/~wangjun/ssi-demo.html

Weismer, G. and Bunton, K. (1999). Influences of pellet markers on speech production behavior: Acoustical and perceptual measures, *Journal of the Acoustical Society of America*, 105: 2882-2891.

Westbury, J. 1994. *X-ray microbeam speech production database user's handbook*. University of Wisconsin-Madison, Madison, Wisconsin.

Author Index